Lives Lived Large

Lives Lived Large

Minnesotans in the Public Eye

Dean Urdahl

NORTH STAR PRESS OF ST. CLOUD, INC.

This book is dedicated to my three sons:
Chad, Brent, and Troy.
May they live their lives large.

All photos provided by subjects.
George "Pinky" Nelson photo courtesy Ron Adams, *West-Central Tribune*.
Gary Paulsen photo courtesy *Random House Children's Books*, by Tim Keating.
Will Steger photo courtesy *Duluth News-Tribune*.

Design: Seal Dwyer

Printed in the United States of America by
Versa Press, Inc.
East Peoria, Illinois 61611

Published by:
North Star Press of St. Cloud, Inc.
P.O. Box 451
St. Cloud, Minnesota 56302

ISBN: 0-87839-164-9

Table of Contents

Foreword vii
Elmer L. Andersen, Governor, Businessman, & Philanthropist 2
Louie Anderson, Entertainer 6
Ann Bancroft, Educator & Explorer 12
Patty Berg, Pro-Golf Hall of Famer 18
Kathleen Blatz, Minnesota Supreme Court Chief Justice 22
Dr. Norman E. Borlaug, Plant Geneticist & Nobel Peace Prize Winner 26
Henry Boucha, Olympian & Pro-Hockey Hall of Famer 32
Herb Brooks, World Championship Hockey Coach 38
Neal Broten, Championship Hockey Player 44
Gretchen Carlson, Miss America & News Anchor 48
Nancy Carlson, Author & Illustrator 52
Herbert Chilstrom, Lutheran Pastor & Bishop 56
Leeann Chin, Restaurateur 62
Orville L. Freeman, Governor & United States Secretary of Agriculture . . 66
Bud Grant, Pro-Football Coach & Athlete 72
Jimmy "Jam" Harris & Terry Lewis, Musicians & Producers 76
Nellie Stone Johnson, Activist 80
Linda Kelsey, Actor 84
Harmon Killebrew, Pro-Baseball Hall of Famer 88
Mike Kingery, Professional Baseball Player 92
Jonny Lang, Musician 96
Tom Lehman, Professional Golfer 100
Eugene McCarthy, United States Senator 106
Kevin McHale, Pro-Basketball Hall of Famer 112
Vern Mikkelsen, Pro-Basketball Hall of Famer 116
Walter F. Mondale, Vice-President & United States Ambassador 122
Dr. John S. Najarian, Transplant Surgeon 126

Lou Nanne, Hockey Player & Businessman 130
George (Pinky) Nelson, Astronaut & Scientist 134
Earl B. Olson, Businessman 138
Lute Olson, National Championship College Basketball Coach 142
Alan C. Page, Minnesota Supreme Court Justice & Pro-Football Hall of Famer . 146
Gary Paulsen, Author 150
Carl Pohlad, Owner of the Minnesota Twins & Banker 154
David Preus, Pastor & Bishop of the American Lutheran Church 158
Kirby Puckett, Pro-Baseball Hall of Famer 162
Harold Stassen, Governor & Statesman 166
Will Steger, Explorer & Educator 172
Bobby Vee, Singer 178
Jesse Ventura, Entertainer & Governor 184
About the Author 189
New London-Spicer Class of 2005 190

Foreword

This book is an attempt to bring the lives of notable Minnesotans into focus for readers of all ages. Those interested in contributions to our history and culture by people with Minnesota ties may gain some insight.

The idea for this book began as a class project at New London-Spicer Middle School in New London, Minnesota, where I teach American History. My seventh-grade students were involved in the research and wrote questions for the people we included. They also suggested many of the people we contacted.

The first question that logically comes to mind is, why are some people included and others not? My students even raised the point of why some people who "aren't famous" are included. In their terms, that is anyone of whom they haven't heard.

The goal was not to include only "famous" people. I explained to my students that, since many other noteworthy individuals have enriched our history and culture, we should hear and learn about them, too.

Let me be a little more specific in explaining our selection process. First, the people had to be alive and able to answer our questionnaires.

People included did not have to be born in Minnesota, but they had to have spent to significant time in our state, and/or have made notable contributions to our culture or history while living here. For example, Dr. Norman Borlaug, winner of the Nobel Peace Prize, was born and bred in Iowa. But he was educated in Minnesota and was an instructor at the University of Minnesota. The training and inspiration he needed to become a prize-winning scientist came from this state.

We sent out about fifty letters. Forty responded. A few said no. Others just didn't answer us, sometimes after repeated attempts to contact them. Sometimes the fate of our project was in the hands of secretaries who were already very busy. For example, Minnesota Twins' employee Glo Westerdahl contacted three members of the Twins for us. It wasn't easy for her to pin down busy people to answer questions for a bunch of seventh graders. I'm grateful for her help. I just didn't dare ask her for more of her time. Thus, Paul Molitor, a likely future member of baseball's hall of fame, isn't in the book.

However, Mike Kingery, a solid major leaguer who certainly deserves to be included, is in this book. He's not a hall of fame prospect, but Mike lives within twenty miles of our school. He was easily accessible and more than willing to help. Accessibility played a big part in this project.

Bobby Vee, Jonny Lang, Jimmy "Jam" Harris, and Terry Lewis are included because they answered us. While we very much wanted Bob Dylan in our book, he was inaccessible.

We found that it was exceptionally difficult to contact and get responses from "Hollywood" Minnesotans, despite our earnest resourcefulness. We are grateful for Louie Anderson's reply.

I have tried to be as accurate as possible and to emphasize positive aspects of our subjects' lives.

Many people ought to receive thanks in an effort of this type. Once again, I often had to work with secretaries to obtain the information I needed. I'd like to thank our school secretary, Connie Lee, for her help in faxing people for me and for putting me through on the telephone. The most frequent words she's ever heard me say are, "Line, please, Connie."

Also, thanks go to our other school secretary, Barb Knisley, and to Superintendent Henry Lubbesmeyer for his support.

My students deserve a large measure of credit for the work they put into this project. Their efforts helped me gain access to people who otherwise would not have been available.

To my family, I reserve the biggest thanks, particularly to my wife, Karen. She provided ideas and support but, most importantly, acted as editor. Our three sons, Chad, Brent, and Troy, were also helpful with suggestions and questions. Chad, a newspaper sports editor, was a valuable resource when Karen needed a sounding board.

And, certainly, genuine thanks go to the people who answered our questionnaires. Some of them put considerable time into their answers to make them as meaningful as they could for the people who will read them. Obviously, there would be no book without the input of these very important people who took the time to care about a bunch of kids from New London-Spicer Middle School.

Lives Lived Large

Elmer L. Andersen
Governor, Businessman, and Philanthropist

He had made a fortune in business and worked for a progressive, modern Minnesota. Elmer L. Andersen, governor of Minnesota from 1961 to 1963, was a man of broad and compassionate interests.

His concerns were varied, and his programs for his state covered a wide spectrum. But Elmer Andersen had time for people. His door was open to his little nieces and nephews, including the offspring of his brother-in-law, State Senator Stanley Holmquist. The children had a free pass to visit Uncle Elmer. The governor was a man who cared about people not just in the broad sense but also in the specific.

Elmer Andersen was born in Chicago in 1909. Then his family moved to Muskegon, Michigan, where young Elmer spent his formative years. He attended school in Muskegon, making spare money by selling newspapers for the *Muskegon Chronicle*.

After high school, he attended junior college. Then, he traveled to Minnesota, North Dakota, Wyoming, and Montana working for a school supply firm.

While still a young man, Andersen set three goals for himself: to own and operate a farm; to serve in the state legislature; and to publish a newspaper. Eventually he accomplished all three.

He made other wise choices first. Elmer married Eleanor Johnson, his devoted partner for over sixty years. He decided to join a small glue company in St. Paul. That company, H. B. Fuller, would grow tremendously and would eventually, with Elmer at the helm, become a major corporation numbering among the Fortune 500 companies. Elmer Andersen's wealth would grow proportionately.

Andersen was elected to the State Senate from his St. Paul district in 1948. He was a progressive, moderate Republican in the mold of the Stassen Republicans of the previous decade. Andersen promoted legislation for special education and handicapped children.

Minnesota's legislature was officially non-partisan in those days. In lieu of party designations, legislators identified their preferences with the brands of Conservative and Liberal. Andersen caucused with the Republican-aligned Conservatives.

He served for ten years, but chose not to run again in 1958. Elmer Andersen had set his sights on another goal: governorship of Minnesota. The sitting governor, Orville Freeman, was in his third two-year term.

Labor and economic problems plagued Freeman in 1959 and opened the way for Andersen in the 1960 election. Democratic presidential candidate John F. Kennedy won Minnesota by 20,000 votes over Republican hopeful Richard Nixon. Elmer L. Andersen became Minnesota's thirtieth governor by an almost identical margin over Freeman.

He was sworn into office on January 4, 1961. Andersen's inaugural address spoke to the needs and problems of the state. He spoke of the needs in Minnesota's agricultural economy. Then he turned his attention to the needs of industrial expansion, iron ore production, forestry, and tourism.

Andersen's message was progressive as he spoke of the importance of education, conservation, and the future of Minnesota's highway system. He gave support to human rights and emphasized housing, employment, and civil liberties. The new governor reminded people of the needs of minorities, including Minnesota's Native American population. His satisfaction came from helping all people in need of help.

The legislative session was partisan. The Democrat-allied Liberals controlled the House, while the Conservatives led the Senate.

A measure that had been pushed by many leaders for years, including previous Governor Freeman, was finally established in 1961. This was a system of "withholding" for the collection of state income taxes. A measure to establish a state sales tax failed; three constitutional amendments were placed before the people; and the prickly problem of reapportionment was handled.

Governor Andersen was most proud of the Taconite Amendment, which aided the iron ore industry and boosted the economy of northeastern Minnesota.

The election campaign of 1962 brought two ways of accomplishing goals before the public. Both the Republican and Democrat parties expressed support for progress and the many issues that Minnesotans cared about. Governor Andersen ran for re-election opposed by then-Lieutenant Governor Karl Rolvaag, who was a Democrat.

But while the Democrats desired to use the "process of government" to pass their programs, the Republicans spoke of "expansion of opportunity." In the last days of the campaign, the DFL party charged that a highway in northern Minnesota was built using improper construction procedures. These charges were eventually shown to be largely unfounded, but they may have turned the tide.

The election was held November 6, 1962. The results of the governor's race were not declared final until more than three weeks later on November 29, when the State Canvassing Board declared that Andersen had been re-elected by 142 votes.

But Rolvaag called for a recount. 96,000 ballots were challenged. On March 15, the judges overseeing the recount declared Rolvaag the winner by ninety-one votes. No election for governor in Minnesota has been closer.

Elmer Andersen was not done serving Minnesota. He would serve other governors of both parties on commissions. He would chair the University of Minnesota Board of Regents and become president of the Child Welfare League of America.

At the age of sixty-seven, Andersen fulfilled another of his lifetime goals by publishing a weekly newspaper. His wide range of interests was revealed in more than 2,000 editorials that he wrote over the next twenty-some years. In 1997 he received the Kay Sexton Award for his "contributions to the Minnesota community of the book."

Elmer Andersen, a man of humble beginnings who became wealthy, was generous not only of his talent and service, but also with his money. He gave generously to many causes and charities, including the Lindbergh Foundation, the Children's Home Society of Minnesota, the University of Minnesota, and, through the influence of his wife, Eleanor, to the arts. He greatly admires his dearest friend, Tom Swain.

The Andersons had three children. The couple lives in Arden Hills, Minnesota.

"My advice to young people is to be aware, to participate, to read newspapers, to join a political party of your choice, to attend caucuses. To be a really serious citizen of the United States, you need to be a participant. You just can't be on the sidelines. And surely the least duty of all citizens is to vote at every election and then to consider your own potential for office holding as a township member, school board member, or whatever. A legislative experience is a wonderful education. Every person has potential far beyond their own belief in themselves. So believe in yourself, strive to be significant and be proud of your country."

Sources: *Minnesota: A History of the State*, by Theodor Blegen, pp. 583-585, University of Minnesota Press, Minneapolis, 1963; *Views from the Publisher's Desk*, by Elmer L. Andersen, Nodin Press, Minneapolis, 1997; interviews with family members.

Louie Anderson

Entertainer

By his own admission, Louie Anderson was an overweight, unhappy youth. He was born on the wrong side of the tracks in the Roosevelt Housing Projects of St. Paul, Minnesota, in 1953. He was the tenth of eleven children. Their alcoholic father was verbally abusive toward them.

Those factors—poverty, a troubled home life, poor self-esteem, and ridicule—are ingredients for failure. It takes a special person to rise above them to success. Louie Anderson did, becoming one of America's foremost comedians.

His father, Louis, had been a musician. A trumpet player with Hoagy Carmichael's band, he played on the original recording of the classic song, "Stardust."

Before Louie was born, his father had to quit his career in music because of his bad teeth. He turned to odd jobs as a railroad detective and a gravedigger.

Louis also drank heavily and used his children as foils for biting, sarcastic humor. Louie's mother helped to hold the family together, and, surprisingly, Louie relays that even though there was much unhappiness, there was a lot of humor, too.

Even his father was funny when he wasn't drinking. Louie would eventually use that humor as a buffer for the ridicule and verbal abuse that would come from neighborhood kids and his family.

In fact, jokes about weight and his father would become the focal points of most of Louie's early humor: "My dad never hit us when I was a kid. He carried a gun."

But Louie didn't start out to become an award-winning comedian. He went to high school in St. Paul and began a career as a counselor for abused children.

His life as an entertainer began by chance. Louie and friends were attending a comedy club in Minneapolis. Louie remarked that he thought he was as funny as the performers. On a dare he took the stage. The excitement and attention were euphoric to Louie.

Louie said later, "With the first laugh, I knew I was hooked, a junkie for life." It was October 10, 1978. Within six months, the young man from St. Paul's East Side quit his job at the children's home to concentrate on writing and performing comedy.

Louie honed his skills, often working local Minnesota clubs for free just to gain the experience and exposure. Eventually he worked professionally at Minnesota colleges. Then he was ready to head to comedy clubs in Chicago and St. Louis.

In 1981 Louie was a winner at the St. Louis Comedy Competition. There he met Henny Youngman and began to write jokes for the famous comedian. The following year, Anderson decided it was time to make his move. He headed west to Los Angeles with six hundred dollars and his 1976 Malibu Classic. Louie was determined to make the big time.

He auditioned at Hollywood's famed Sunset Strip Comedy Store and became a featured regular there. By 1984, he was appearing in Las Vegas, Atlantic City, and other major clubs around the United States. His unique self-deprecating, personal humor delighted audiences everywhere.

His career was growing, but the dramatic boost came on November 20, 1984, when he made his debut on "The Tonight Show" with Johnny Carson. Johnny called Louie out for a rare second bow.

Ironically, watching the "Tonight Show" was about the only thing that Louie and his father had enjoyed doing together. Louis was a big fan of Johnny's musician, Doc Severinson. And Louie admired Johnny Carson.

The comedian hoped to land a deal with a network, but failing that, he returned to Minneapolis in 1985. There he produced his own comedy special, which was sold to Showtime. His special claimed the highest ratings that month for the cable network.

Proving his widespread appeal, his career expanded. Louie appeared many times on television shows hosted by the likes of Arsenio Hall, Jay Leno, David Letterman, Pat Sajak, and Joan Rivers.

He landed parts in several feature films, *Coming to America*, *Quicksilver*, and *Ratboy*. He appeared on TV shows including *Grace Under Fire* and *Remington Steele*, as well as other HBO and Showtime specials.

Success had arrived. Louie was making $40,000 a night for performances around the country. Las Vegas casinos and clubs welcomed him regularly. But something was missing.

Louie felt a need to express his feelings to his father. Louis Anderson had died in 1979, but Louie still needed an outlet for his long-suppressed emotions. While on tour with Roseanne Arnold, he began to keep a diary of letters to his deceased father. In 1988 *People* magazine published one of the letters.

The response from fans was tremendous. The letters were published in a book, *Dear Dad-Letters from an Adult Child*. It became a national best seller, focusing on relationships with alcoholic parents.

His mother died suddenly in 1990. The loss affected Louie deeply. The result was another book of self-examination and evaluation, *Good-bye Jumbo, Hello Cruel World*.

Louie brought to television the pain and humor of his childhood in the animated Fox series, *Life with Louie*, which he created along with Matt O'Callahan. The show was launched as a Christmas special in 1994 and continued as a series on Saturday mornings from 1995 to 1998.

Life with Louie showcased Louie's stand-up comedic talent, writing and voice-overs, but it also had a message for kids. The series dealt with themes such as ridicule, death, and friends moving away: topics faced by young Louie and other kids in life.

The series was a critical hit. It was 1995's number-one rated animated program. It earned two Emmys for Louie in the category of Outstanding Performance in an Animated Series in the second and third seasons.

Life with Louie also garnered three consecutive Humanitas Prizes and a Genesis Award for the ethical treatment of animals. Despite its success, the series was cancelled in 1998. Louie hopes to eventually revive the program after rights for it revert to him.

Louie based himself out of Las Vegas. He traveled throughout America performing in concert halls and comedy clubs to sold out, enthusiastic audiences. Then, in 1998, he moved to Los Angeles where his life took another turn, one that would bring Louie more satisfaction and happiness than he had experienced during much of his career.

Louie was asked to host a revival of the old game show, *Family Feud*. While producing the *Feud*, his schedule is hectic and the work is demanding; but Louie Anderson claims that he's never been happier, thanks, in part, to the show.

The entertainer from St. Paul resides in Beverly Hills. However, Louie's memories of Minnesota, his childhood, and thoughts of today's kids are never far away. Throughout his life, Louie has shown kids that they don't have to have perfect bodies to succeed and be accepted, but that it helps to care about others and to be able to look with humor for the child within us all. Being so successful has its ups and downs. Louie enjoys having people know and recognize him, but he does not like it when they try to use his fame to push their own issues.

"The advice I have for you is to be a good and loyal friend. Find something you love to do, something that makes you happy, and learn to do it as well as you can. Be the best you can at it. Most of all, follow your heart. If you do this you can't go wrong. Don't do what everyone else does; do what you believe in."

Sources: Information provided by Louzell Productions, *Minnesota Monthly*, February 2000 article, *Life with Louie,* by Russell Scott Smith, Comedians USA Website.

Ann Bancroft

Educator and Explorer

Richard and Deborah Bancroft recognized their daughter Ann's adventurous spirit when she was young. They encouraged her to reach high, not knowing what she might achieve, and she heeded that advice. Ann would gain fame as an explorer of the frozen poles of the Earth, an unlikely legacy for a struggling student who wanted to live in Africa. Ann Bancroft achieved far beyond most people's expectations.

Born on September 29, 1955, Ann was raised in her family's old farmhouse near Mendota Heights, Minnesota. She loved the great outdoors. With her two brothers and two sisters, she spent hours roaming the fields near their farm.

Ann started school at Somerset Elementary in Mendota Heights. When schoolwork proved difficult for her, Ann's parents transferred her to Summit School in St. Paul. They hoped that the private school would be able to help Ann with her problems in learning. However, the change in schools didn't help. Neither did tutoring.

Only in gym class did Ann excel. There her competitive, adventurous spirit was set free in sports. A natural athlete, Ann found that the failures of the classroom could be forgotten on the playground.

Her life changed dramatically when her father, an insurance agent, quit his job to do missionary work for their church. The Bancroft family was bound for Kenya in Africa.

For the next two years, the Bancrofts lived and worked on the "Dark Continent." Ann grew to love it there and wouldn't have complained if her family had stayed permanently.

However, for her seventh-grade year, they returned to Minnesota. Ann enrolled at St. Paul Academy and found that school was even harder for her. Then tests revealed that Ann was dyslexic. Her brain signals mixed up numbers and letters and made it difficult for her to put them in the proper order.

Identifying the problem was important, but it didn't make things easier for her. During Ann's junior year, she transferred to Henry Sibley High School in St. Paul. There she excelled in track.

Ann created another outlet for her sports abilities by organizing her own basketball team. In the early 1970s in Minnesota, high-school sports were just beginning for girls. Many schools didn't have basketball or other sports for girls.

During summers Bancroft found the most happiness. Then she attended, and later worked at, summer camps in northern Minnesota. She was in her element helping to teach camping and canoeing.

Ann enjoyed teaching others about camping and athletic activities so much that she decided to attend college and become a teacher. In spite of her poor academic record in high school, the University of Wyoming accepted Ann.

After high school, Ann and four young women from her camp went on a two-month-long canoe trip. Then it was time to venture west. She loved the mountains and played field hockey, basketball, and softball in college.

After Ann's second year in Wyoming, her parents' house in Minnesota burned down. She returned home to help her family.

That winter they returned to Kenya. With her brother Bill, Ann climbed Mt. Kenya. She fell in love with adventure and mountains.

When some of her sports programs were dropped, Ann decided to leave Wyoming. She stayed near mountains, however, at the University of Oregon. She graduated with a degree in physical education and returned to Minnesota, where she became athletic director and a physical education teacher at St. James School in St. Paul.

For two years, Bancroft taught at St. James School. She also moonlighted, working in a mountaineering store as she prepared to climb Mt. McKinley in June of 1983.

America's highest peak, McKinley rises 20,320 feet. Ann and a friend, Tim Elgren, began their ascent on June first. By June 18, they made it to the top. But Tim was in bad shape, suffering from hypothermia. Without Ann's guidance and care, he would certainly have perished, but his friend brought him down the mountain safely.

For the next two years, Ann Bancroft taught at the Clara Barton Open School. Then Will Steger called, and her life changed forever.

Steger was already a noted explorer and outdoorsman. He had met Dick Bancroft on a winter camping trip at the Minnesota Outward Bound School. Will kept in touch with the Bancrofts off and on over the years. Although he didn't know Ann well, he knew of her mountain climbing and outdoor pursuits.

Steger was impressed with her efforts to save Elgren on Mt. McKinley. In the summer of 1985, Will was planning a historic expedition. His team's goal was to reach the North Pole by dog sled without resupply.

One of Steger's team members had dropped out of the expedition because of a knee injury. A replacement had to be chosen. Will literally dreamed that Ann should be on the team, so, late in August, he asked Ann to his base camp near Ely and invited her to join the expedition. She readily accepted.

For a year they trained. On March 8, 1986, seven men and one woman, Ann Bancroft, began their long journey by dog sled. They would depend on three tons of supplies they brought with them; there would be no airlifts or resupply. Their goal was to retrace the effort of immortal explorer Robert Pearey, who had traveled in a similar manner in 1909.

Ann was Will's dog sled partner and also served as first-aid agent for the expedition. Steger was particularly impressed by how quickly Ann adapted to sledding and by the affection and compassion she showed for the dogs.

Reading material was limited on the journey. One team member took a small *New Testament*. Ann took Viktor Frankl's *Man's Search for Meaning*, a book about a Jewish survivor of Hitler's death camps. As the pages were read, they were ripped out to start the camp stove.

For fifty-five days they braved temperatures of seventy degrees below zero, deep crevasses, icy water, frozen clothing, and frostbite. Ann fell through a crack in the ice and plunged waist-deep into the freezing ocean water. Only by flinging her arms spread-eagle was she able to keep from sinking deeper.

The team kept going with remarkable perseverance. The harrowing journey was an incredible success. On May 1, 1986, they reached the North Pole. Ann Bancroft became the first woman to achieve this hallmark in exploration history, the first woman in history to travel over the ice to the North Pole.

Ann didn't return to teaching in schools. She was named *Ms. Magazine's* Woman of the Year for 1987 and came into great demand as a speaker. She maintained an interest in outdoor programs for disadvantaged youth and led canoe trips.

But the exploration bug had bitten. The polar regions kept calling. In 1993 Ann led the American Women's Expedition to the South Pole, a sixty-seven-day expedition of 660 miles on skis. This made her the first woman to have traveled over ice to both poles.

Ann was inducted into the National Women's Hall of Fame in 1995. She founded and still leads the Ann Bancroft Foundation, a nonprofit organization focused on celebrating the existing and potential achievements of women and girls.

The lure of adventure and the poles keep pulling Ann back. On November 13, 2000, she and Liv Arnesen of Oslo, Norway, began the first all-women's crossing of the Antarctic landmass. They pulled 250-pound sleds while skiing 2,688 miles across the continent.

Ann and Liv completed the arduous journey on February 12, 2001, reaching the Ross Ice Shelf ninety days after beginning their trek.

Ever the teachers, they presented an innovative educational program, via the internet, as they traversed the frozen continent. While they awaited an airplane that would take them from the ice shelf to the American base at McMurdo Station, the two explorers linked up to a class of third graders in Faribault, Minnesota, and conversed with the kids about their experience.

For Ann, the projects that involve students bring the most satisfaction. Ann sees the enormous polar regions as "expanses of white in every direction." To share this with kids across the country has been very rewarding. Her advice to school children is, "Know that many of your dreams can come true with hard work, support from others, and perseverance."

Sources: *North to the Pole,* by Will Steger, Times Books, New York, 1987; *Ann Bancroft, On Top of the World,* by Dorothy Wenzel, Dillon Press, Minneapolis, 1990; biographical data provided by Global education *www.yourexpedition.com.*

Patty Berg
Pro-Golf Hall of Famer

If one asks Patty Berg to emphasize the superlatives in her life, she won't, even though she is one of the greatest female golfers in the history of the sport. The GolfWeb chart of the Ladies Professional Golf Association (LPGA) has a category indicating when the golfer joined the organization. For Patty Berg, the chart says "Founder."

Patty would rather credit other people for accomplishments in forming the LPGA and in playing golf. She is modest to a fault, but the life she lived broke ground for women and sports. Patty's role was that of a historic pioneer. She is an extraordinary athlete who strongly believes in giving back to her sport and to society.

She was born Patricia Jane Berg in Minneapolis on February 13, 1918. She loved all kinds of sports and even quarterbacked the "Fiftieth Street Tigers," a neighborhood football team that featured future legendary football coach Bud Wilkinson at tackle. She also excelled at baseball.

Patty might have chosen other paths. She was a natural athlete, showing great prowess in high-school track and speed skating. In fact, she won the midget speed skating championship of Minnesota the first time she entered. The next year, Patty placed third in a national skating competition.

But golf became an early love. Prompted by her father, Herman, a Minneapolis grain broker, and by her brother, Patty started playing at the age of thirteen. Three years later, she won the 1934 Minneapolis City Championship. This was the first of twenty-eight amateur championships over seven years.

Her victories included three Titleholders (1937 to 1939), the 1938 U. S. Amateur, 1938 Western Amateur, 1938 and 1939 Trans-Mississippi Championship, 1938 Western Derby, and five Helen Lee Doherty Championships (1936 to 1940). In 1936 and 1938, Patty played for the U.S. Curtis Cup Team.

Many of these victories occurred while she was attending the University of Minnesota, where she had enrolled in 1938 after completing high school in Minneapolis.

Her amateur career quickly turned into a dazzling success. At age seventeen, she was a virtual unknown outside of Minnesota. By the time she turned twenty in 1938, Patty had won every major amateur golf title. That year (1938) Berg was named the Associated Press' Athlete of the Year. She gained the AP honor twice more, in 1943 and in 1955.

Patty Berg turned professional in June of 1940. The next year, she won her first professional tourney, the Western Open. Fifty-six others would follow.

She also began a long-time association with Wilson Sporting Goods Company. Patty's duties with Wilson were largely educational, appearing at summer camps for girls and golf-coaching schools.

There were interruptions to her career. From 1942 to 1945, Patty served as a lieutenant in the Marine Corps in World War II. Unfortunately, illness and injuries were also frequent companions. She was sidelined eighteen months after a car crash in 1941. Several operations forced her to take time off, too: cancer surgery in 1971, major hip surgery in 1980, and back surgery in 1989. And sometimes, as she has described it, she just had the "awful awfuls." But Patty's tenacious attitude helped her return to the links each time.

Ms. Berg's first six professional victories came before the Women's Professional Golf Association was formed in 1946.

One of her greatest years, 1948, marked a significant one for women's golf, too. Patty won seven tournaments and also became a founder and charter member of the LPGA during that year.

Intensity was a hallmark of her play. Sportswriters of the day likened Patty's competitive spirit to that of golfing great Bobby Jones and boxer Gene Tunney.

Over the next fourteen years, she won forty-four titles while serving as the first LPGA president. She dominated women's golf in the 1940s and 1950s, gaining fifteen major championship titles. In 1953 she totaled seven victories; in 1955 she earned six, and in 1957 she had five. Patty won the *Golf Digest* Performance Average Award three times, for 1953, 1955, and 1956. During the 1959 U.S. Women's Open at Churchill Valley Country Club in Pittsburgh, Berg became the first woman to record a hole-in-one in United States Golf Association competition.

Berg was the LPGA money leader in 1954, 1955, and 1957. Her career earnings on the tour were $190,760. Due to the loss of early LPGA records, Patty's actual career earnings were greater. However, in today's economy her purses would have been phenomenal. Like every other sport, golf has become bigger in every way.

Patty's last tour appearance was in 1980. She wrote three books on golf and continued to practice faithfully after ending her appearances on the tour. In the summer of 1991, she shot a hole-in-one at the age of seventy-three.

Berg lives in Fort Myers, Florida. Retirement is not a term that would describe her life in the South. Giving back to her sport and to society remains an important part of Patty Berg's life. She continues to golf and to actively promote it. She works to help children. She works for many charities including cerebral palsy and cancer. The University of Minnesota has the Patty Berg Development Fund.

Patty Berg is deserving of many honors and recognition. A multitude of awards has come her way. She is one of only two women to gain entrance into the PGA Hall of Fame. Berg has been inducted into many other halls of fame, including those of the LPGA, Women's Sports, the PGA World Golf, the University of Minnesota, the American, the Minnesota, and the Florida Sports Hall of Fame.

But perhaps even more meaningful to Patty are the numerous awards that include descriptions like humanitarian, contributor, teacher, and meritorious. Whether on a plaque or not, those words describe the life and achievements of Patty Berg, a woman whose life should serve as an example for anyone wishing to rise above personal adversity to success, distinguished service, and courage.

Patty's advice to school children is, "Stay in school, be serious about learning, be truthful and fair in your dealings with others, and don't be afraid to dream big dreams."

Sources: *Current Biography 1940*, Maxine Block, Editor, pp. 75-77, H. W. Wilson Company, New York, 1940; LPGA Website.

Kathleen Blatz
Minnesota Supreme Court Chief Justice

Kathleen Blatz learned about public service as a young girl. As she campaigned for her father, State Senator Jerome Blatz, she probably didn't realize where it all could lead. But the message of service she gained from her parents was ingrained early, and, by the age of twenty-four, Kathleen was a state representative.

Blatz was born in 1954 and raised in Bloomington. She attended high school at the Academy of Holy Angels and went on to the University of Notre Dame in South Bend, Indiana, where she graduated in 1976. Then she returned to her home state for post-graduate studies and received a master of social work degree from the University of Minnesota in 1978.

However, the political bug that bit when she was a child campaigning in her dad's Bloomington-Richfield district had caught hold. So in 1978, she ran as an Independent-Republican candidate for the House of Representatives from a district in Bloomington. She was successful. Kathleen served fifteen years.

As a legislator, she made the needs of at-risk children and their families a priority. Representative Blatz served on various committees, including taxes, judiciary, rules and administration, and health and human services. She also chaired the Crime and Family Law Committee, was co-chair of the Minnesota Task Force on Youth Service Work, and was an important part of the Child Protection System Study Commission.

Representative Blatz wanted Minnesota to become more responsive to the needs of modern families. She was proud to have sponsored the "Cocaine Baby Law" to address the problems of "crack" babies. She also authored a law creating a Children's Trust Fund and numerous laws to protect children.

State Senator Steve Dille, who served with Kathleen in the Minnesota House, was impressed with her grasp on issues. Senator Dille commented, "She was always attentive in committee meetings, not reading the paper or mail. Kathleen was all business."

During her legislative career, Blatz attended law school, earning her law degree from the University of Minnesota in 1984. She rose in leadership in her caucus, serving as assistant minority leader from 1987 to 1990 and 1992 to 1994.

Kathleen was also in private practice as an attorney with the firm of Popham, Haik, Schnobrich, & Kaufman, Ltd. From 1992 to 1993, she served as Assistant Hennepin County Attorney.

Blatz's legislative career ended in 1994, during the middle of her eighth term, when she was appointed District Court Judge for the Fourth Judicial District. Her time in District Court brought Kathleen into direct contact with many of the serious social and criminal issues facing society and families today. She dealt with cases involving substance abuse, child protection, child custody, and juvenile delinquency.

Kathleen served only three years on the District Court bench, for, in November of 1996, Governor Arne Carlson appointed her Associate Justice of the Minnesota State Supreme Court. In this role, she also served on the Governor's Task Force on Fetal Alcohol Syndrome, helping to make the public more aware of the effects that drinking while pregnant can have on fetuses.

Just two years later, Kathleen Blatz became the first female Chief Justice of the State Supreme Court when Carlson chose her to succeed retiring Chief Justice A.M. "Sandy" Keith.

Justice Blatz responded to the appointment by saying, "I have a great interest in the court system's response to the challenges faced by families and children. But justice is bigger than any one court system, which means we have to work together. Families in Minnesota need to know that we are willing to form partnerships with schools, faith communities, businesses, and social service agencies to provide local support and early intervention. We can have an incredible impact if we pull in the same direction."

The *Minneapolis Star-Tribune* commended Blatz's appointment, saying, " . . . an ingenious choice for chief justice. Every year the courts see more families at the breaking point, more juveniles lapsing into criminality, more children suffering at their parents' hands. To respond thoughtfully to these crises, the court will need tremendous insight and sensitivity. It will need Kathleen Blatz, who can do both."

During her term on the Supreme Court, Justice Blatz has continued to place issues involving children and families in the forefront. She has pushed the effort to open juvenile protection hearings to the public.

The Chief Justice has broken molds and established firsts for much of her career. She has had an impact on all three of Minnesota's branches of government. As the head of Minnesota's top court, she continues to work for the people of her state in the best way she knows how.

Throughout her life, Kathleen has consistently emphasized helping people who are vulnerable and need help in strengthening the family. Whether a social worker, legislator, lawyer, judge, or Chief Justice, she hasn't wavered in her concerns.

Blatz is married to Tom Berklemen. The couple has three sons.

Blatz's advice for school children is: "Study hard! Education is something that nobody can take away from you, and it prepares you for life's choices that you don't even know you will want to make some day. We all have different potentials and we all have different talents, but what we share in common is our need to be educated and well rounded. The Minnesota school system offers you that opportunity, but it is your individual responsibility to take advantage of it. Good luck!"

To Blatz, role models are of singular importance. "The primary roadblock that I experienced was that in many areas there were not as many women role models to help guide one's professional development. Today the world of politics looks very different in that more women have been elected to city councils, school boards, county boards, and the legislature, as well as statewide office. Until the election in 2000, however, we have not had a woman represent Minnesota congressional districts since United States Congresswoman Coya Knutson, who represented Minnesota from 1955 to 1959." In 2000, Betty McCollum was elected to Congress from St. Paul.

Justices, as opposed to the community of legislators, are solitary in their decision-making. In fact, justices are prohibited from discussing any pending case. Decisions hardest to make are those requiring the creation of new statutes—statutes without ambiguity. All people are granted a fair trial. Many changes need to be made to courts to equalize the pressure of efficiency versus effectiveness. Blatz gained re-election in 2000. It was her wish to help the courts move forward.

One of Blatz's mentors, her aunt Sister Camille Bowe showed her an example of great care for people. "She truly had an interest in everyone she met."

Sources: Biographical materials provided by Minnesota Supreme Court; interviews with colleagues.

Dr. Norman E. Borlaug
Plant Geneticist and Nobel Peace Prize Winner

The word "revolutionary" brings many historical figures to mind, from Juarez to Lenin, Castro, Sun Yat Sin, or Sam Adams. It conjures visions of war and mayhem.

In 1942, a revolutionary earned his third degree from the University of Minnesota. But his would not be a war against oppressive governments. He wouldn't head an army of desperate soldiers. His revolution would be called "Green," and it would earn him one of the highest honors offered in this world, the Nobel Peace Prize.

His name was Dr. Norman E. Borlaug. Just as determined as the driven revolutionaries of history, Borlaug had a vision to fight hunger and to help the world's underdeveloped countries feed themselves.

Borlaug was born in the tiny Norwegian community (now extinct) of Saude, Iowa, near Cresco, on March 25, 1914. The oldest of three children, he was raised on his father's small grain and dairy farm.

Norman was a bright boy, but he was held back a year before attending a nearby one-room schoolhouse. While in high school, he was a member of the football, basketball, and Cresco's famous wrestling team. He graduated from Cresco High School and then, short of money, he stayed home a year to work. Borlaug wanted to teach and coach. He planned to attend Iowa State Teachers College. But a chance visit by a family friend, George Champlin, who played halfback for the University of Minnesota, resulted in Norman's traveling north to Minneapolis to enroll at that university.

Borlaug worked toward a degree in forestry and also wrestled for the university. During this era, freshmen were not permitted to compete in intercollegiate competitions in any sport.

However, during this time an All-University Tournament in all individual sports was held. Borlaug won both the 145-pound and heavyweight championships. During his sophomore year, he won eight out of nine matches.

At the beginning of his junior year, Dave Bartelma, his coach at Cresco High School, became the wrestling coach at the University of Minnesota. The new University of Minnesota coach wanted to start a high-school wrestling program in

Minnesota, for it was virtually nonexistent. To that end, he sent Borlaug and another wrestler around the state to meet with parents and teachers and to give wrestling demonstrations.

The forestry major from Iowa was instrumental in starting wrestling as a high-school sport in Minnesota. While in graduate school, Borlaug retained his ties with the sport and served as an assistant wrestling coach.

But all experiences in Minnesota were not pleasant for Norman Borlaug.

For the first time, in the fall of 1933, the boy from northeast Iowa was exposed to the horrid Depression-era conditions of a big city. It was in Minneapolis that the fire within Borlaug to ease world hunger was kindled.

He saw huge numbers of unemployed people begging for food, hungry and sleeping in the streets. Young Borlaug witnessed farmers losing their land and the consequent sheriff's sales.

In need of money in 1935, Borlaug interrupted his education to supervise emergency work programs in soil conservation and forestry. First hand, he endured the "Dust Bowl" and the effects of erosion.

During the fall quarter of 1937, Borlaug had another experience that changed his life. He attended a Sigma Xi lecture by Dr. E.C. Stakman, head of plant pathology at the university. The world described by Stakman fascinated Borlaug. He began to think more seriously about graduate school and studying under Stakman.

Fate entered. The job with the Forest Service that Borlaug expected was delayed due to budgetary problems. He went to graduate school, where he earned a master's degree in plant pathology in 1940 and a Ph.D. in 1942.

Borlaug had worked off and on for the Forest Service and was touched by the condition of the young men with whom he worked. He related, "I saw young men, seventeen or eighteen years old, arrive at the Civilian Conservation Corps (C.C.C.) camps hungry and malnourished. At the camps, they were able to recover some semblance of health and self-confidence. I saw how food changed them."

Feeding the hungry would become his life's work. While at the university, he met Margaret, his future wife and supporter in a crusade to save the world from overpopulation.

He worked briefly for DuPont and then went to Mexico in 1944 to work with the Cooperative Mexican Government-Rockefeller Foundation Agricultural Program, which evolved into the International Maize and Wheat Improvement Center (CIMMYT).

The goal was to expand food production. Mexican agriculture was a disaster. The soil was dry and exhausted, fertilizers were hardly used. Insects and disease, particularly rust, cut deeply into yields. Mexican wheat production was less than twelve bushels per acre. They had to import ten million bushels a year, over half of what was needed. Dr. Borlaug chose to tackle the task of increasing wheat yield first.

Several problems presented themselves. Wheat rust in the summer was a killer. The tall wheat stems would break in wind and rain, losing the head of grain. Organic fertilizers required animals that used land desperately needed for crops.

For twenty years, Borlaug and his crew labored over these problems and others. They had to try to make genetic matches to find a stronger, better strain of wheat. Each season Borlaug's crew made from 2,000 to 6,000 individual cross matches.

Each year they studied the performances of 40,000 varieties of wheat. It took thirteen years to get the rust problem under control, but yields were still low.

Then came a breakthrough. Norin, a dwarf variety of wheat from Japan, became the last part of the puzzle for Borlaug's miracle. This stunted plant had a shorter, thicker stem able to withstand wind and rain.

By raising Norin, Mexican farmers were able to increase yields up to 105 bushels per acre. In four years, instead of importing half the wheat needed, Mexico was able to feed its people and export surplus wheat.

Next, Borlaug turned his sights on other areas where exploding populations were fast outrunning the ability of countries to feed their people. India and Pakistan experienced situations similar to what Mexico had seen. In 1963 Borlaug visited the two countries.

Rice was the staple there, not wheat. But, in 1965, the two governments were so impressed with the results from test plots of dwarf wheat that they ordered 700 tons of seed. In India, agricultural production would eventually increase from 200 to 600 percent. By 1999, wheat yields had grown in India to seventy-three million tons, up from eleven million in 1963. Similar fantastic increases in wheat production soon followed in Pakistan, Turkey, China, Argentina, Brazil, and Chile.

Work was also begun to increase rice production as well through better genetic varieties and crop-management practices.

Norman Borlaug had launched a "Green Revolution," a war against war by fighting hunger, one of the main causes of hostilities. The scientist said, "My interest is broader than food. It's what it can do for people. Miserably hungry people are not very pleasant to be with, and you can't have peace for long without food."

In 1970, the Nobel Prize Committee agreed with him. He was awarded the Nobel Prize for Peace. Typically, Borlaug was in the field, about thirty-five miles from Mexico City, when word arrived via telephone.

So Margaret Borlaug drove an office car out to the field to inform her husband that someone from Oslo had called and said he had won the Peace Prize. Borlaug thought it was a joke and went on with his work.

An hour and one-half, later a journalist drove up with teletype proof that Margaret had been right. This time, Borlaug was convinced.

But the Nobel Peace Prize winner didn't rest on his laurels. There was still much of the world to feed. Africa became the next focus for his work. Although he announced a retirement in 1979, Borlaug didn't really halt his work; he just modified his routine.

When the World Bank and the Rockefeller and Ford foundations backed away from his African projects, he found a benefactor in Ryoichi Sasakawa, of Japan, who, along with former President Jimmy Carter, was campaigning for food aid to Africa.

Africa presented a struggle in which Borlaug had to fight resistance to change as well as critics. Still, during the 1995-1996 season, Ethiopia recorded the greatest harvests of major crops in its history, a thirty-two percent increase in production.

Because of his dedication to field work, Norman and Margaret have spent little time in America since 1944. Their two children were born in Mexico.

But dedication to field research has allowed him to see the changes in the United States, not all of which are flattering. "After World War II, the United States had developed into the world's greatest political, industrial, agricultural, and economic power. Our democratic traditions, hard work, educational system, and inventiveness were the envy of the world. Now, when I return home, I see a United States afflicted with the debilitating co-viruses of affluence and complacency."

The Borlaugs did slightly modify their lives in 1980, when Dr. Borlaug began to teach one semester a year during the fall terms.

For the first year, Dr. Borlaug returned to the University of Minnesota to teach. That was followed by three years at Cornell. Since 1986 he has taught at Texas A&M. The Borlaugs bought a house near Dallas and, for the last several years, Margaret has stayed there while Norman returns to Mexico and Africa.

Other honors have come. He was inducted into the National Collegiate Wrestling Hall of Fame and the University of Minnesota Hall of Fame, where Borlaug Hall stands in testament to him.

But one honor will always stand out. Norman Borlaug started the Green Revolution by tenacious wrestling against world hunger, and for that he won the greatest prize of all, the Nobel Prize for Peace.

Dr. Borlaug's passion is apparent. "It is my firm belief that all who are born into this world have the basic right not only to food, but to the other essentials for a decent humane life. This means access to food, clothing, adequate housing, education for the young, basic medical care, and above all, opportunity for gainful employment."

Dr. Borlaug's advice to school children: "I try to challenge young students to utilize their years in universities to the fullest to develop the potential talents inherited from their parents, grandparents, and great-grandparents. I challenge them not to be satisfied with mediocrity."

Sources: *Living History Interview* with Dr. Norman E. Borlaug, University of Iowa College of Law, 1991; *Minnesota Magazine*, "Raising the World's Grain," as told to Vicki Stavig, July-August 1996, pp. 23-25; *The Lutheran Standard*, "No. 1 Hunger," by Russell B. Helgesen, May 4, 1973, pp. 2-6.

Henry Boucha
Olympian and Pro-Hockey Hall of Famer

The coach looked down the bench at his players. The fans in the packed high-school ice arena screamed encouragement. Because of a penalty and exhausted players, the Warroad Warriors were in desperate need of a defenseman.

A young Native American boy, an eighth grader, sat near the end of the bench. He gazed expectantly at his coach, who motioned him onto the ice. Roseau, the archrival, had the man advantage. The young player handled the puck at his own blue line. As an opposing player closed in on him, the boy coolly spun away and skated to center ice before lobbing the puck deep into the zone.

His moves were like those of a veteran, but hockey fans in Warroad, Minnesota, weren't surprised. They had been watching Henry Boucha play youth hockey for years. They knew what he could do.

Henry was born in 1951, the son of a French-Canadian-Ojibway father, George, and an Ojibway mother, Alice. George was a Canadian fisherman and logger. Alice was an American-Canadian treaty Indian from Buffalo Point, Canada. When Henry was a few years old, the family (George was the eighth of nine children) moved to the little town of Warroad, on the south shore of the Lake of the Woods. The big lake was divided between the United States and Canada.

Things went smoothly at first. Fishing was good. Henry played hockey on the ponds and rivers. The older boys let him play goal when they were short of players. The youngster excelled at the position.

Then, in 1957, government regulations turned disastrous for the Boucha family. The Canadian government outlawed gill netting in Buffalo Bay, Manitoba. Since George was not a citizen of the United States, he couldn't get a fishing license for the U.S. side. The Boucha family faced economic peril that plagued them for years.

But kind people in Warroad helped Henry. If he needed skates or other equipment, someone would come through for him. They liked to watch the young boy play.

In youth hockey, he played for both the peewee and bantam teams at the same time, skating "out" for the younger team and playing in goal for the twelve- and thirteen-year-old boys. The bantam team went on to win the 1964 Bantam State Hockey Championship by defeating a Twin Cities suburban hockey power, Edina.

After his auspicious beginning against Roseau, Boucha launched a magical high-school career. Three times he was named to the All-State Hockey Team. He also excelled as a track sprinter, football place-kicker, and power-hitting baseball player.

Too valuable and swift a skater to stay a goalie, Henry was made a defenseman and later a forward. Boucha was magnificent to watch as he glided down the ice. His coach said that Henry could turn on a dime and reach full speed in two strides.

One goal had escaped him. The Warriors had not reached the Minnesota High School Hockey Tournament, widely considered the premier high-school sports event in America. But, during his senior year, they finally made it.

In 1969, Warroad High School, with fewer than 200 students, went to the Met Center to challenge the big schools in a one-class tournament.

They beat Minneapolis Southwest and Roseau. In each game, Henry scored the winning goal in the third period. That set the stage for a classic match between little Warroad and the powerful team from the prosperous suburb of Edina.

The game was fast and hard-hitting. In the second period, Edina held a 2-1 lead when a collision with an Edina defenseman sent Henry hurtling into the Plexiglas. Boucha was out of the game with a concussion and a broken eardrum.

After a valiant comeback by Warroad, Edina prevailed 5-4 in overtime. The people of Warroad raised $1,500 to pay Henry's hospital bill.

The following fall, Henry was set to attend the University of Minnesota. Then, in early September, he abruptly changed his mind and signed to play Junior A Hockey with the Winnipeg Jets of the Western Canada Hockey League. It was in this league where he encountered problems because he was "not only American, but an American Indian." He described the league as not as "gentlemanly" as high school.

Henry was barely eighteen when he returned to Warroad that October to marry a girl he had been dating since eighth grade, Debby Bleau.

The Warroad youth also had dreams for his longtime sports love, hockey. He wanted to play in the National Hockey League some day, but first he wanted to follow the path of Warroad hockey legends Billy and Roger Christian to the Olympics.

During his season with Winnipeg, Murray Williamson, coach of the U.S. National Team, asked Henry to try out for the squad. He made the team and played the 1970 season with them. At the conclusion of the national team's schedule, Henry managed to get back to Winnipeg to close out the hockey season with the Jets in their playoffs.

Boucha entered the army and divided the next year and one-half between the military and playing hockey for his country as his army duty. After another season on the national team, he fulfilled a lifelong goal in 1972, when he was named to the United States Olympic squad. The team wasn't expected to do much, but Coach Williamson instilled a fiery desire in his players. Henry led the team in scoring as the young Olympians surprised everyone by winning a silver medal in Sapporo, Japan.

Also in 1972, Boucha was drafted in the second round and sixteenth overall by the Detroit Red Wings. He finished up the year playing in Detroit, scoring a goal in his first National Hockey League (NHL) game. The next season he sputtered a bit and divided time between the big club and seven games with the Tidewater Wings of Norfolk, Virginia, a minor-league team.

Being demoted seemed to wake him up. Henry played well the second half of the season with Detroit. He was named Detroit's Rookie of the Year and set a NHL record for the fastest goal when he scored in just six seconds against Montreal on January 23, 1973.

As his hockey world brightened, Henry's personal life took a tumble. His tumultuous marriage to Debby ended as she took their baby daughter, Tara, and returned to Warroad.

His marriage had been a financial strain, and Henry struggled to mend his finances. He ran camps for young players in the summer and worked hard at hockey.

Henry thought that Detroit would be his longtime hockey home, but at the start of the 1974-1975 season he was traded to the Minnesota North Stars. Minnesota fans were excited about the return of the high-school legend. He had developed into a colorful player.

Henry had all the skills, the graceful stride, explosive speed, and rocket shot. He wore his black hair long and affected a headband. While Henry maintained it was to keep his hair in place and the sweat from his eyes, fans couldn't help but attach Native American significance to the headgear. Boucha didn't discourage the notion. He even marketed headbands in pro shops.

It seemed that he was on the verge of fulfilling the great promise within him. He was making better money, $105,000 a year with the Stars; he had begun a caring relationship with a young woman named Randi Peterson; and he was back in his home state, where people loved him.

Then tragedy struck and his world came tumbling down.

On January 4, 1975, the North Stars were playing the Boston Bruins, a team known for thuggish play. Dave Forbes was shadowing Henry, baiting him, slashing with his stick whenever Henry touched the puck. They fought. Tempers were short.

When they hit the ice after a penalty, Forbes charged Boucha. Henry had looked away and didn't see the Bruin coming. Forbes rammed the butt end of his stick into Henry's right eye. The result was thirty stitches and permanent damage to the eye. From that moment on, Boucha would see double.

Henry tried to play at the end of the season, but he just couldn't see well enough. In total, he had eye surgery three times to reconstruct the eye socket. Nothing could restore what he had lost.

After brief attempts at comebacks with the Minnesota Fighting Saints in St. Paul and teams in Kansas City and Colorado from 1975 to 1977, Henry Boucha gave up playing hockey. He was just twenty-six years old.

The life and promise on which Henry had always dreamed were gone. Minnesota's Hennepin County charged Dave Forbes with assault, but he was not convicted. Henry did receive a settlement from the NHL, the Bruins, and Forbes.

Henry married Randi in May 1975, about four months after his career-ending injury, and they had two children. But he grew bitter about the tragedy and its resolution, and it affected his marriage, which ended in 1979.

Henry wandered. Business ventures in Washington State and Detroit failed. He wound up living in Idaho, where he hunted, fished, and grieved for his lost life. Then Henry met Elaine, a woman who shared his love of the outdoors and helped him to find purpose and motivation once again. They were married in 1982.

In 1986 Henry and Elaine returned to Warroad. Henry was determined to be successful again, as a person and in business. He went to work in real estate and founded an Indian education program in the Warroad Public Schools.

Boucha was determined to help Native American kids who needed assistance, who had problems at home and in school, kids like he had been. With that goal in mind, he founded Kah-bay-kah-nong in 1998. The nonprofit agency provides fundraising and management for Boucha's various interests, which range from an annual Warroad powwow to an Indian youth hockey program.

Henry also coaches youth hockey, including a team that numbers among its players J.P. Boucha, his twelve-year-old son. In 1995, Henry was inducted into the U.S. Hockey Hall of Fame.

Henry Boucha's life is in order; it has a center once again as the former hockey great has devoted himself to his family and the roots from whence he came.

We can measure the man by how he recovered after he hit bottom, and by what has become important to his life. Perhaps his young son Jean Paul, then age seven, best expressed what his father has become when he wrote, "Daddy wants me to be a nice boy and grow up right. Daddy takes me hunting and fishing; in the winter we go ice fishing. We go houseboating, and we explore the islands and look for eagle feathers and old Indian stuff like arrowheads and pots. It is hard. I love my daddy because he loves me and takes care of me."

It's a fine yardstick for a man.

The game has changed since Boucha played. It has come to rely too heavily on stick work. He also believes that violence should be dealt with strongly.

"The greatest satisfaction in life is helping people. You are born with nothing, and you go out with nothing. It is what you do while you are here, that matters. It has nothing to do with money or material things. The Great Spirit has seven laws of creation according to the Ojibway: love, kindness, sharing, respect, truth, courage, and humility."

Henry's advice for school children is, "Don't ever quit because opportunities will always come."

Sources: *Henry Boucha, Star of the North*, by Mary Halverson Schofield, Snowshoe Press, Edina, Minnesota. 1999; *American Indian Lives*, by Nathan Aaseng, *Facts on File*, New York, June 1995; *Minnesota's 20th Century*, by D.J. Tice, University of Minnesota Press, in cooperation with the *St. Paul Pioneer Press*, 1999; *When I Think About My Father, Sons and Daughters Remember*, by Mary Kay Shanley, Sta-Kris Inc., Marshalltown Iowa, 1996; author's phone conversation with Henry Boucha.

Herb Brooks
World Championship Hockey Coach

Herb Brooks' life has been hockey. The icy trail he chiseled took him to the peak of success as a coach and player. But after Stanley Cup playoffs, Olympics, and Final Fours, Brooks says his greatest satisfaction comes from teaching and helping young players achieve their goals.

He's a man who took the time, when visiting a hockey rink that impressed him, to seek out the custodian to compliment him on his fine maintenance.

Brooks was born in St. Paul, Minnesota, in 1938. He started skating when he was four or five years old and played through youth hockey programs. His father most influenced him to become a coach.

Herb's hockey road took him through high school at St. Paul Johnson and the Minnesota State High School Hockey Tournament, one of the foremost high-school events in America.

As a player, Brooks was a three-year letter winner at the University of Minnesota. Five times he represented the United States on the National team. He played twice on the U.S. Olympic hockey team, in 1964 and 1968. He was the captain of the 1965, 1967, and 1970 National teams, and was a co-captain on the 1968 Olympic team.

Before signing on to coach the 1980 U.S. Olympic squad, Brooks spent seven years at the helm of the University of Minnesota's Golden Gophers hockey team. Those seasons under Brooks were the best in the school's history. Herb led the Gophers to five winning campaigns, five WCHA titles, and three NCAA championships.

It is the Olympics, however, that will forever meld Brooks with one of the greatest moments in American hockey. Herb Brooks coached the 1980 "Miracle on Ice" team to the Olympic gold medal.

He brought together a team, the majority of it Minnesotans, that challenged some of the greatest teams in the world in what many consider the world's greatest sporting event at Lake Placid, New York.

The first game was against Sweden. Between periods of a tight game, one of Brooks' University of Minnesota players, Rob McClanahan, complained of a thigh injury. Rob questioned his ability to play the rest of the game. According to Olympic teammate Phil Verchota, Brooks was livid.

"He got all over Rob," Verchota recalled. "He shouted, 'You'll be in there! Sitting out is not an option. You will play!'"

Verchota described his coach as a taskmaster, a hands-on leader who focused on the game and not the social aspects of coaching. He was all of that at the 1980 Olympics. The Swedish game ended in a tie.

The medal round matched the Americans against the dreaded Russian team. Only thirteen days earlier, the USSR had crushed the Americans 10-3 in a game played at Madison Square Garden in New York City. Many acknowledged that the Russians were the best team in the world, better than the best professional teams in the National Hockey League.

But Brooks kept insisting that the Russian team was ripe for an upset. The U.S. Olympic hockey players averaged just over twenty-one years of age. Wearing his gold blazer, Herb addressed the young squad in the locker room before the game.

"You were born to be a player," he told each young man. "You were meant to be here. This moment is yours."

The Russians jumped ahead in the first period 2-1 as they outplayed the young Americans. Then, in the final second of the period, Mark Johnson slipped the puck past the Russian star goalie, Tritiak.

In the second period, the Russians outshot the Americans 12-2 and took a 3-2 lead. History was made in the third. Mark Johnson scored his second goal about midway through the period. Eighty-one seconds later, Mike Eruzione fired "the shot heard 'round the world" when he fired one by the Russian netminder.

The impossible had happened. Herb Brooks had coached a bunch of young college kids to victory over the team that many considered the world's best. Electrified, the crowd chanted thunderously, "USA! USA!"

The thrilling upset lifted the U.S. Olympic hockey team to the gold-medal game. Twenty years later, that victory over the Soviets was named by *Sports Illustrated Magazine* as the "Most Memorable Sporting Event of the Twentieth Century."

But it wasn't over. The Americans still had to beat Finland. Prior to the gold-medal game, Brooks was intense. He told his players, "Gentlemen, if you lose this game, you'll take it to your grave."

They didn't lose. It took two late goals. One was the tying marker by Phil Verchota. America won the Olympic Gold Medal, topping Finland. Once again the fans chanted with wild excitement, "USA! USA!" Preserved for posterity, the historic scene is replayed often each day at Disney World's Epcot Center, in the U.S. pavilion's recap of highlights in our nation's history. Brooks remembers a soft feeling of peace of mind at the win.

Herb Brooks went to Europe to coach in 1980-1981. The next year he returned to the United States and was named head coach of the New York Rangers for the 1981-1982 season.

Brooks coached the Rangers for three and one-half seasons. His team's record under his tenure was 131 wins, 113 losses and forty-one ties. New York made the playoffs three times. Herb's 131 wins and .532 winning percentage are fourth best in Ranger history. The national publication *Sporting News* named the Minnesotan its "Coach of the Year" after the 1982 season.

Brooks was lured to St. Cloud State, Minnesota, for the 1986-1987 season. In his one year with the Division III team, the Huskies posted a 25-10-1 record and made it to the national Division III Final Four. Brooks was instrumental in putting the team on course to become a Division I program.

Bill Frantti, long-time Minnesota hockey coach, helped bring Brooks to St. Cloud. He noted, "Herbie appreciates people who do a good job and who go above and beyond what's expected of them. He's all business, no nonsense until the job is done."

Then Brooks returned to the NHL. He coached the Minnesota North Stars in 1987-1988. Next, he served as a commentator for *SportsChannel America* for two years before coaching Utica of the American Hockey League for one year.

Brooks was inducted into the U.S. Hockey Hall of Fame in Eveleth, Minnesota, in 1990. But his contributions to the sport were to continue.

Brooks was named head coach of the New Jersey Devils for 1991-1992. The Devils finished 40-37-7 and made the NHL playoffs. April 26 of 1993 marked his last game with New Jersey. Brooks thought his NHL coaching days were over.

He became a Pittsburgh Penguins' scout and returned to the Olympics in Nagano, Japan, as head coach of the French hockey team in 1998. Afterward,

Brooks returned to Minnesota, where he did some sports broadcasting and toyed with thoughts of running for Congress.

Then his old friend Craig Patrick, assistant on the 1980 Olympic team and current general manager of the Penguins, called Herb back to the NHL. At age sixty-two, Brooks took over the reins of the Pittsburgh Penguins midway through the 1999-2000 season.

Brooks left the Penguins after that season and took on another challenge. He became the coach of the United States Olympic team for the 2002 games. The man who helped make the miracle happen decided to seek another.

Herb still makes his home in St. Paul. He and his wife, Patti, have one son, Dan, and a daughter, Kelly. He says that more ex-players need to come back and reinvest in the coaching of youth.

Sources: Pittsburgh Penguins Web site; interviews with acquaintances.

Neal Broten
Championship Hockey Player

The crowd counted down the final seconds: "Three, two, one!" A horn blasted, and the throng screamed, "USA! USA!" One of the red, white, and blue-clad hockey players skated toward the center of the rink and jubilantly flung his stick end-over-end, high into the air.

Neal Broten was experiencing the greatest moment of his hockey life. The United States had just won a game deemed by many to be the greatest single sports contest of the century, and in doing so had captured the 1980 Olympic Gold Medal.

Just south of the Canadian border, in the small Minnesota town of Roseau, one of the most storied careers in American hockey was launched twenty years earlier. The spectators at the frozen ponds and ice arenas of the northland town were the first to witness the magic that would amaze hockey fans worldwide.

Neal was born November 29, 1959. Hockey became an early passion. As he scored six, seven, or eight goals per game in peewee games, his skills and potential became obvious to everyone. With his brothers, Paul and Aaron, and best friend, Butsy Erickson, he honed his talents with early morning practices and countless "shinney" hockey pick-up games.

The hours and work would lead to a career in hockey that no American has ever matched. It included three appearances in the Minnesota State High School Hockey Tournament, an NCAA National Championship, the first-ever Hobey Baker Award (given to the best college hockey player in the country), an Olympic Gold Medal, and three appearances in the Stanley Cup Finals, the last one yielding a championship.

All this from a player only five feet, nine inches tall and 175 pounds.

While Neal was dedicated to helping his Roseau Rams win a state championship, he led a well-rounded life growing up. In the summers, he often took a break from hockey and played golf. He felt that it was not good to be consumed by one sport while in high school.

Unfortunately, getting close was all the Rams could do when Neal played for them. They didn't win a state championship in his four years on the team.

After a semi-final state tourney loss in 1978, Broten announced that he would attend the University of Minnesota. In his freshman year, he scored twenty-one goals and had fifty assists for the Golden Gopher hockey team. The fifty assists broke a twenty-five-year-old record at the "U." Neal was named the WCHA's Rookie of the Year for the 1978-1979 season.

The Gophers, under Coach Herb Brooks, won the NCAA Championship that year. It was the first big plum of Neal Broten's career.

More successes would quickly follow. In the 1979-1980 season, he was named to the U.S. National Team. This led to Lake Placid and the "Miracle on Ice" Gold-Medal victory in the 1980 Olympics.

After the historic wins over the Russians and Finns at Lake Placid, Neal could have turned professional, for he had been drafted by the Minnesota North Stars. However, he opted to return for another year at the University of Minnesota.

He notched seventy-one points in the 1980-1981 season, but the Gophers lost in the NCAA finals. Broten joined the North Stars after his final Gopher game and played the last three regular-season games, scoring a goal in his first pro game.

Once again Broten's timing was amazing. He had come to the North Stars just in time for their first run to the Stanley Cup Finals. The North Stars lost to the New York Islanders in five games.

For twelve more seasons, Neal Broten, wearing jersey number 7, would excite the devoted hockey fans at the Met Sports Center in Bloomington, Minnesota. Later, he played two-plus seasons in Dallas after the Stars moved to Texas.

Neal holds or shares twelve Stars franchise records. Two times he represented Minnesota as an NHL All-Star. From 1981 to 1986, he was the North Stars' top scorer with 425 points. In 1986, Neal became the first American player to score over one hundred points when he totaled 105.

He led Minnesota to another Stanley Cup Final in 1991. This time, the Pittsburgh Penguins eliminated the Stars in six games.

One of the Broten family's highlights occurred in March of 1990. On a weekend when the Roseau Rams won the state high school hockey championship, the North Stars held "Broten Brothers Day."

In another memorable family event, a pro hockey game played at the Met Sports Center featured three Brotens. Neal and Aaron played for the Stars. They faced their brother Paul, a member of the New York Rangers.

After the 1992-1993 season, the Stars left Minnesota. Neal played with them for two years in Dallas. During the 1994-1995 campaign, he was traded to the New Jersey Devils. It was just in time for another Stanley Cup run. This time Neal's team came out on top, as Broten scored two goals in the championship game to clinch the victory. The Roseau native savored the magical thrill of winning Lord Stanley's Cup and of skating with it during the on-ice celebration that followed.

The next season Neal played with the Devils again. In what would be his final NHL season, 1996-1997, his time was divided between four teams: New Jersey, the Los Angeles Kings, eleven games with the IHL Phoenix Roadrunners, and a return to the Dallas Stars.

Neal Broten finished his career second to Joe Mullen for the most games played by a U.S.-born player with 1,099. When he retired, he ranked fifty-ninth all-time in the NHL in points at 923 and forty-second all-time career NHL assists at 634.

Neal finished his career as an active player with service on the 1998 United States Select Team, joining brothers Paul and Aaron on the squad. In April of 1997, he was named to the all-time USA Hockey First Team.

Neal was honored by twice winning the Lester Patrick Award, which is given for outstanding service to hockey in the United States.

Even though his playing days are over, hockey is still in Neal Broten's blood. He continued his involvement in the sport he loves by working with promotions for the Minnesota Wild, Minnesota's re-entry into the NHL.

Otherwise, Neal enjoys time with his wife, Sally, and their daughters, Brooke and Larissa, on their seventy-five-acre horse ranch near River Falls, Wisconsin.

The days of precision slap shots and deft passes are over for Neal Broten. The golf club now swings in his hands more than a hockey stick, and his gold medal resides in a dresser drawer. But the challenge of helping to build a new franchise remains, and the boy from Roseau is part of it.

His advice to school children is, "School is much more important than sports. Work hard at school. Get the best education you can."

Sources: Biographical information provided by Minnesota Wild; *Frozen Memories* by Ross Bernstein, p. 79, Nordin Press, Minneapolis, 1999.

Gretchen Carlson
Miss America and News Anchor

Gretchen Carlson, by her own admission, was a chubby youth. She spent hours upon hours practicing to be a classical violinist. Eventually she decided not to make the violin her life's profession. But the training and discipline provided by years in music led her to Atlantic City, New Jersey, and aided in her eventual occupation.

Gretchen Carlson was born in Anoka, Minnesota, on June 21, 1966, to Lee and Karen Carlson. Her childhood was normal except that she had a remarkable gift. She played the violin very well and worked hard at it. Gretchen was offered a prestigious Julliard School of Music scholarship.

Carlson worked hard at her violin as she grew up. However, as she prepared to graduate from Anoka High School in 1984, she decided that too many things in life interested her beyond music. Gretchen chose to give up music as a career and enrolled at Stanford University in California. During her junior year in 1987, she studied at Oxford University in England.

But her parents were reluctant for her to completely abandon something to which Gretchen had devoted so much time and talent. They urged their daughter to find other ways to make use of her violin talent.

Gretchen's mother, after receiving a pamphlet in the mail, suggested the Miss America Organization. She noted that fifty percent of a contestant's points were based on talent. Gretchen decided to go for it without holding back.

After becoming Miss Minnesota in June of 1988, she temporarily dropped out of Stanford to put a one-hundred percent effort into the Miss America contest.

Gretchen practiced her violin, worked out, and tried to prepare for the interview phase by reading and talking to people. At the same time as Miss Minnesota, she also was required to represent the state organization at community events and parades.

Having drive, determination, and self-discipline paid off for Gretchen Carlson. At Atlantic City, she won the crown of Miss America 1989. She became the first classical violinist, and the third Miss Minnesota, to be so honored.

Being crowned launched Gretchen on an exhausting year of travel and public appearances throughout the nation. She promoted the importance of education, the fine arts, and goal-setting.

Whereas many professional athletes and performers resent the tag of "role model," Gretchen embraced it. She wanted young people, especially girls, to realize that a once-chubby teenager from Minnesota could meet challenges and succeed, not just on good looks, but with talent as well.

Gretchen pushed to have the swimsuit category of competition pulled from the show. However, the television viewers liked watching that part of the show so much that the swimsuit contest remains.

Upon completing her reign, Gretchen Carlson continued her education at Stanford and graduated in 1990. A career in broadcast journalism was her chosen field.

But she remained thankful for what the years with her violin had taught her. Gretchen stated, "Though I didn't choose music as my career, the discipline I learned from it helps me every day in my career now in television."

Gretchen has gained experience while moving through several television markets. She was a free-lance news reporter at KSTP-TV in Minneapolis, political reporter at WRIC-TV in Richmond, Virginia, and news reporter for WCPO-TV in Cincinnati, Ohio, as well as a main anchor/reporter for CBS in Cleveland, Ohio.

In December of 1998, she was employed as a weekend anchor/reporter for KXAS-TV, the NBC station in Dallas-Fort Worth, Texas.

Gretchen married Casey Close in her hometown of Anoka on October 4, 1997. Revealing a deep sense of family, Gretchen chose to have her wedding ceremony take place in the church where her grandfather had ministered for thirty-five years, and she chose her grandfather to perform the ceremony.

Many honors in broadcasting have been awarded to Gretchen. They include an American Women in Radio and Television National Award in 1997 ("Day Care Security Investigation"), two Ohio Press Club Awards in 1997 ("Best Newscast in Ohio" and "Best Public Service Report"), and Emmy Awards in 1996 and 1994 ("Major League Baseball World Series" anchor and "Best Series").

She also received an American Woman in Radio and Television National Award in 2000 for a thirty-part series on domestic violence.

Gretchen Carlson and her husband live in the Dallas-Fort Worth area.

"During my year as Miss America, mothers of little girls would often ask me whether they should get their daughters involved in pageants, and I would always say, never at a young age. I feel it is very important to make sure entering a pageant is a young woman's decision. For children, I feel it is extremely important to play the piano, play another instrument, or play a particular sport. Through this, kids learn that when you practice something you get better at it . . . and you learn discipline from applying yourself to something. This develops who a child is on the "inside" first, instead of putting all of the importance on the outside."

Gretchen's favorite memories from her reign were "meeting the president in the Oval Office, being on *Hollywood Squares* and *Bloopers and Practical Jokes,* performing my violin, playing the national anthem for *Monday Night Football.*"

Source: Biographical information provided by subject; personal interview by author; Miss America Website; KXAS Website.

Nancy Carlson
Author and Illustrator

The little girl knew when she was in kindergarten that she wanted to make pictures when she grew up. It's quite amazing to know your life's work when you're only five years old, but Nancy Carlson did. So while she read the Besty-Tacy books by Maud Heart Lovelace, she dreamed of her own books.

Nancy is a lifelong Minnesotan. She was born October 10, 1953, to Walter and Louise Carlson in Edina. She attended school in Edina and then the University of Minnesota in 1972 and 1973. Nancy continued her schooling at the Santa Fe Workshop of Contemporary Art in 1975. She graduated from the Minneapolis College of Art and Design with a major in printmaking in 1976.

Nancy had always wanted to be an artist. She began to illustrate books by other authors soon after graduation. Soon realizing that she would rather illustrate books that she had written herself, Nancy began to do precisely that.

So began the series about a somewhat self-conscious, occasionally insecure dog named Harriet and her family. The first book in the series was *Harriet's Recital* in 1982. Four other Harriet books followed. Nancy created other book series about Loudmouth George and Louanne Pig. But Harriet is her favorite.

Her stories and drawings usually have animals as their main characters, frequently dogs. The books are short, illustrated in vivid colors and usually have brief texts of a sentence or two on each page.

The books convey essential messages for today's kids. Carlson believes " . . . life is fun and should be fun for everyone, including children."

Consequently, her characters aren't perfect. They have fears, anxieties, and disabilities. Through her books, kids learn to cope with their own personal problems. They can learn that kids don't have to be perfect to be good people and to have fun.

Nancy conveys moral messages as well. But the messages are not "preachy." Rather, they gently remind children what is right. She writes about relationships between friends and family members.

Harriet has been described as "every child," someone with whom all kids can identify. That is likely what has made her so popular.

Nancy Carlson has had over thirty-five books published. It takes her six months to write and illustrate one of her books. Nancy loves to illustrate her books best, and when she is doing final art for one of her books, she does not want to do anything but draw. Although aimed primarily at young readers, her stories and artwork have inspired adults as well.

Nancy's favorite of her books is *I Like Me.* Her ideas come from everywhere.

While the author touches many lives through her books, she's not content to just leave it at that. Carlson also reaches out through personal appearances. She frequently appears in schools, where she lectures, demonstrates, and works with kids.

Carlson has received the Children's Choice Award from the International Reading Association and Children's Book Council.

Perhaps Nancy Carlson's books and devotion to young people will help to spawn a whole new generation of writers, with dogs as main characters, of course.

Carlson married Barry McCool, a graphic designer, on June 30, 1979. They have three children, Kelly, John, and Michael, and reside in Bloomington, Minnesota. They also have a cabin on a lake in northern Wisconsin.

Nancy loves the outdoors. She enjoys running, hiking, biking, swimming, and skiing. She also found much enjoyment watching her children participating in sports.

Nancy's advice for school children is, "If kids want to write or illustrate they should practice every day. They should also read a lot. Then go to college, keep writing, keep drawing, and develop a style. Then get out in the world and write, write, write, or do art. Then see what happens. Good luck future authors."

Sources: Biographical material provided by subject; *Contemporary Authors*, Jeff Chapman and John D. Jorgenson Editors, pp. 80-83, Gail Research publishers, Detroit, 1997.

Herbert Chilstrom

Lutheran Pastor and Bishop

The young boy had come to Green Lake Bible Camp in Spicer, Minnesota, to have fun and maybe even get to know pretty girls from other towns. He had just finished ninth grade in his hometown of Litchfield, Minnesota, and had recently been confirmed there at First Lutheran Church.

Gazing into the clear, blue-green waters of Green Lake brought more than just visions of young girls to Herbert Chilstrom. His stay at Bible Camp also had an impact he hadn't foreseen, a week of intense soul-searching, a time to think about his life and his relationship to Jesus Christ.

By the end of the week, he was strongly considering becoming a pastor some day. His camp experience had helped to set Herb Chilstrom upon a path that he would follow the rest of his life, a path that would take him to the pinnacle of leadership in America's Lutheran Church.

Born in Litchfield in 1931, Chilstrom spent his first four years on a farm outside that town. He was baptized at Beckville Lutheran, a picturesque white-clapboard church established by Swedish pioneers, although services were in English.

Chilstrom's father, Walfred, a third generation Swedish-American, was employed by the Works Progress Administration during the Depression and later worked as a church janitor. Walfred and wife, Ruth, raised eight children: six girls, two boys—Herbert and Dave, born with a birth defect.

As a boy, Herb admired the people in his church who took an interest in his friends and Franklin Roosevelt, who led the nation through most of World War II.

In 1949, Herb graduated from Litchfield High School at age seventeen. He moved to Minneapolis, home of Augsburg College, and earned a bachelor of arts degree from the Lutheran college in 1954. He married Corine Hansen on June 12, 1954.

Now Chilstrom was ready to prepare for the ministry. He attended Augustana Seminary, receiving a master's degree in theology four years later in 1958. Pastor Chilstrom began his ministerial service at Augustana Lutheran Church in Elizabeth and Faith Lutheran Church in Pelican Rapids, Minnesota.

Chilstrom moved into the realm of education in 1962, serving as professor and dean at Luther College in Teaneck, New Jersey. During this time, he also achieved a master's degree in theology from Princeton Seminary.

He was called back to parish ministry to be senior pastor at First Lutheran Church in St. Peter, Minnesota, in 1970. But his tenure in that capacity would be relatively short lived.

Chilstrom's stature in the Lutheran Church in America continued to grow. He earned a doctorate of education from New York University. Then, in 1976, he was elected Bishop of the Minnesota Synod of the LCA.

Bishop Chilstrom stated that he never asked anyone to vote for him. He never campaigned for office. He just "let things happen."

Bishop Chilstrom presided over enormous transition in the Lutheran Church. The winds of change led to a historic merger when the Lutheran Church in America, the American Lutheran Church, and the Association of Evangelical Lutheran Churches in America joined, creating the Evangelical Lutheran Church in America (ELCA). Chilstrom noted that more mergers are not likely, as it is too costly and time-consuming.

In 1987, the ELCA named Herbert Chilstrom its first presiding bishop, the head of five and one-half million Lutherans.

The bishop urged the church to reach out, not worried that full communion with other Protestant denominations would weaken the Lutheran identity of the ELCA. Bishop Chilstrom said, "Our church has deep roots in the Protestant Reformation. We won't forget our identity as we seek greater fellowship with other Christians."

Chilstrom worked during his tenure to establish an identity for the ELCA. "We need to continue the quest for greater visible unity among believers and together we need to share the essence of the gospel. In other words, fellowship and witness."

The ministry has changed over the years, especially in two ways: women now commonly work outside the home, requiring churches no longer to depend on women being free to do the kinds of volunteer work they did in the churches fifty years ago; now, ELCA women can be ordained. Without them, the ELCA would have a critical shortage of pastors.

Chilstrom strode with conviction onto the stage of world religious leadership. He served on the board of directors of the Lutheran World Federation as vice-president. He had an audience with Pope John Paul II in 1987. As presiding bishop, he continued to work closely with his churches to reach out with Christian mission.

Of all the world leaders, Chilstrom believes that Jimmy Carter promoted Christian values the best.

Many honors came Chilstrom's way. He was awarded honorary degrees from fourteen colleges and seminaries, the Augsburg Medal from Augsburg College, the Royal Order of the North Star by King Carl Gustav of Sweden, the Fine Arts Award from Gustavus Adolphus College, and the Pope John XXIII Award, from Viterbo College.

But perhaps the greatest honors have come from those who have known him best: the people of his hometown and the pastors with whom Chilstrom has worked. First Lutheran Church in Litchfield, where he was confirmed, named its new fellowship hall "Chilstrom Hall" in recognition of his service.

Pastor Daniel Buendorf of First Lutheran said of Bishop Chilstrom, "He's one of the kindest, most thoughtful, learned, most unpretentious bishops I've ever met. He's a true people-person, deserving of much human respect."

Corine Chilstrom also was ordained into the ministry. The couple raised three children: Mary, Christopher, and Andrew.

Retirement years have found Herb and Corine dividing their time between their lake home at Pelican Rapids, Minnesota, and their winter home in Green Valley, Arizona. Leisure pursuits include gardening, photography, golf, fishing, hunting, and travel. From time to time, they return to Herb's native Litchfield, where his brother, Dave, a retired nursing home janitor, lives.

Chilstrom reflected, "Before church people can pretend to be proclaimers of hope and judgment, they must first see themselves as ordinary people. Distinctive honors have come my way. But when my head gets too large, it's time to go back to my hometown. There are still folks there who call me 'Herbie.'"

Even though the bishop has enjoyed high honors in his life, his greatest satisfaction came from being pastor and sharing God's message with other Christians.

In 1992, the bishop's hometown honored him by naming him grand marshal of the town's summer Watercade celebration.

It was an honor Chilstrom chose to share. Seated next to the tall, white-haired, distinguished-looking bishop, as the parade unfolded through throngs of spectators packed along the route, was his brother, Dave.

Chilstrom's advice for school children is, "Decide now who you want to be and begin to think about what you want to do with your life. I'm not suggesting that one must be a Christian in order for life to make sense. I've known Jews, Muslims, and even agnostics who have led very happy, productive lives. But for me, keeping Christ at the center has been the key to a life that has been as rich and exciting as anything that I could ever have imagined."

Sources: *The Lutheran Standard; Minneapolis Star Tribune;* interviews.

Leeann Chin

Restaurateur

The little girl's fingers were lightning quick as she totaled the day's receipts on her father's abacus. A crowd gathered to watch, amazed at how speedily she worked.

It was 1944. Little eleven-year-old Leeann had hurried from school to her father's market in busy Canton, China, to deliver rice on bicycle, order spices, rice, and herbs, and help with the calculations.

Because preparing good food was an early interest for Leeann, she spent spare time in the family kitchen, experimenting with recipes and questioning the family chef. She could hardly know that some day she would head a food empire with fifty-seven locations in faraway Minnesota.

American-made movies fascinated the young girl, particularly the freedom with which Americans seemed to enjoy their lives on film. She became a bride, marrying Tony in 1951 when she was just eighteen. Life in China left few options because of governmental turmoil, and Leeann had married into an very traditional family that believed women should not work outside the home. The call of a better life in America burned into Leeann's mind and wouldn't let go.

In 1956 she and her husband left Hong Kong for Minneapolis, Minnesota. Leeann had a sister living in Minneapolis willing to "sponsor" them. Ms. Chin left with hope but not much more. She couldn't speak a word of English.

Raising five children in a new land was hard, prompting Leeann to seek ways to supplement the family income. For twenty years, she operated a sewing and alterations business in her home. She also worked on her English.

Sometimes Ms. Chin would serve dinner to her customers and friends. "Soon I was being asked over and over for the recipes of the food I prepared at these dinners," Leeann said. Thus started a new phase in her career. In 1972, she began teaching cooking classes in homes and schools. This grew into party, banquet, and reception catering.

In 1980 General Mills published *Betty Crocker's Chinese Cookbook Recipes by Leeann Chin*. It contained many of the recipes from her cooking classes. A second book, *Betty Crocker's New Chinese Cookbook, Recipes by Leeann Chin*, followed in 1990.

A dinner that she catered in 1980 became a turning point in her career. The dinner was for Minnesota Twins' owner Carl Pohlad. In attendance was the famous actor, James Bond himself, Sean Connery. Both men were so impressed that they became early investors in Leeann Chin's first restaurant.

Ms. Chin was prepared to work hard. She knew how to buy produce and was familiar with equipment dealers because of her cooking classes and catering.

Her idea was to offer the authentic Szechwan and Cantonese cuisine of her homeland, Canton, China. Getting the financing for the venture was a stumbling block, especially for a woman from China with little formal education and no support from her husband.

Enter Pohlad, Connery, and other investors. With their help, a Small Business Administration loan, and her own contribution, her business was launched with a restaurant in the Bonaventure Shopping Mall in Minnetonka, Minnesota.

The restaurant's immediate popularity soon led to expansion to other locations. In 1985 Ms. Chin sold the business to General Mills, but she re-acquired it three years later. She explored other areas of expansion, including a partnership with the Byerly's supermarket chain. The business continues to prosper and grow. Changes over the years have been drastic—everything is computerized.

Leeann Chin feels blessed. She also feels an obligation to give back to the community that supported her. "I believe you have to care about the people around you if you want to have them care about you," she said. "It's important to me to be known as a good human being."

Leeann Chin has shown she cares by tireless efforts for her community. She serves on the boards of directors of the College of St. Benedict, the Boy Scouts of America, the Lowertown Redevelopment Corporation, and the Minnesota Vikings Advisory Board. She is a member of the Committee of One Hundred, a national organization giving voice to Chinese-Americans. She has served on numerous other boards and founded the Leeann Chin Foundation in 1995. Headed by her daughter, Laura Chin, the foundation donates to various events and functions in the community.

Despite her financial success, she says that her children and grandchildren are her greatest achievement.

Leeann advises school children to "get a good education. This is so very important."

Source: Biographical material provided by subject.

Orville L. Freeman
Governor and U.S. Secretary of Agriculture

Orville Freeman worked closely with the pioneers of modern Minnesota politics to forge one of the most powerful political machines in Minnesota. Then he went on to achieve national distinction in elective and appointive office.

Freeman was born in Minneapolis on May 9, 1918, to Orville and Frances Freeman. He attended the University of Minnesota, where he earned a bachelor of arts degree and Phi Beta Kappa honors in 1940. Freeman continued his studies at the university by entering its law school.

Growing up, Freeman idolized sports stars. "Bronco Nagurski, the great football player, was a great role model to many of us as were a number of baseball players, such as Babe Ruth and Lou Gehrig. A professor at the University of Minnesota Political Science Department, Everett Kirkpatrick, and one of my classmates who was several years older than me, Hubert Humphrey, were considerable role models and leaders to me as I began to consider while in college what I wanted to do when I grew up."

But World War II interrupted his pursuit of a law degree. Freeman volunteered for the Marine Corps in 1940. As a second lieutenant, he fought with valor. He was seriously injured while on patrol on a South Pacific island when, in a Japanese ambush, he was shot in the neck and jaw. Freeman was awarded the Purple Heart and discharged as a major.

Freeman returned to Minneapolis and law school in 1945. He graduated in 1947 and began the private practice of law.

In the mid-1940s, he came into close contact with many people who would dominate future state and national politics. Among them were Don Fraser, future mayor of Minneapolis and congressman; Eugenie Anderson, who would become the first woman ambassador in United States history as ambassador to Denmark; Art Naftalin, future mayor of Minneapolis; and future U.S. senators and vice-presidents, Walter Mondale and Hubert Humphrey.

This group helped to forge the Democrat Party, once an also-ran third party in Minnesota, into a union with the Farmer Labor Party. Dubbed the Democratic-Farmer-Labor (DFL) Party, it eventually dominated state politics.

Orville began his career in public service when Minneapolis Mayor Hubert Humphrey appointed him as an assistant in charge of veterans' affairs.

There were early failures. After becoming DFL Party chairman in 1948, Freeman lost bids to become Minnesota attorney general in 1950 and governor in 1952.

Freeman was involved in national politics as well. The 1948 Democratic National Convention focused the national spotlight on Minnesota during the struggle over seating of delegates and platform issues involving civil rights issues.

Minneapolis Mayor Hubert Humphrey made a memorable speech, urging his party to "march forthrightly in the sunshine of civil rights." Freeman, among others, fought to ensure full participatory rights of all Americans in national Democrat conventions.

Freeman made his second run for governor in 1954. This time, he defeated incumbent Republican C. Elmer Anderson to break seventeen years of Republican control over the state house. Eyes were on the former Minneapolis attorney as he set out to prove that Democrats could manage state government.

Freeman turned out to be an able governor. Many of his programs became law. They included providing for state income tax withholding to ensure a stable system of financing of necessary government services, such as education. His tax proposals called for higher inheritance and gift taxes, expanding the tobacco tax, increasing taxes on the earnings of telephone companies, and raising taxes on beer and iron ore.

Freeman was deeply involved in expanding support for the University of Minnesota and all higher education. Many of his advisors came directly from the "U."

The new governor also called for a Water Resources Board and approved measures providing Social Security coverage for state and local employees. His administration established the Metropolitan Planning Commission in order to increase understanding of the problems of the Twin Cities metropolitan area.

Governor Freeman spoke out for working people and strongly supported organized labor in numerous ways, including recognizing the American Federation of State, County and Municipal Employees (AFSCME) as the bargaining agent for state employees. He strove to make government more efficient by reducing the number of boards and commissions.

An other concern of Freeman's administration: improving hospitals that cared for indigent and mentally handicapped persons.

At that time, gubernatorial terms were two years. Governor Freeman was up for re-election in 1956 and won, even though Republican president Dwight Eisenhower carried Minnesota for the second time over Democratic challenger Adlai Stevenson.

In 1958 the governor won again. But economic problems mounted in the state. His third term was marred by controversy amid economic and labor troubles.

A steel strike led to a disastrous reduction in iron ore production. Thousands on Minnesota's Iron Range were unemployed. A transit strike in the Twin Cities was also divisive. But the Albert Lea strike of meat packers was most ominous. Governor Freeman declared martial law in Albert Lea and closed the meat packing plant to ease the threat of violence.

Fortunately, no one was killed. But sending the National Guard to be on duty on the streets of the southern Minnesota city was met with much criticism. A federal court condemned the action and ordered the plant reopened.

In 1960 Minnesota narrowly voted for Democrat John Kennedy in the race against Republican Richard Nixon. But for governor, by only 20,000 votes, Minnesota returned control of that office to the Republicans in the person of Elmer L. Andersen.

Three factors primarily contributed to Freeman's defeat: the economic recession of 1959 led to an increase in taxes in Minnesota; the disastrous labor strike in Albert Lea; and Minnesota's resistance to electing a governor to a fourth term. No Minnesota governor had ever been elected more than three times.

Orville Freeman had worked hard to promote Kennedy for president, giving his nomination speech at the 1960 Democratic National Convention. His hard work, loyalty, and skill were rewarded when President Kennedy tapped the former Minnesota governor to be his secretary of agriculture in January of 1961.

Freeman served President Kennedy and later President Lyndon Johnson in the cabinet from 1961 to 1969. As secretary of agriculture, Freeman helped write farm bills that enabled farmers to get more money for their work, supported agricultural research, advocated the use of America's food surplus to feed the hungry throughout the whole world, and worked towards expanding the marketing of food worldwide.

Freeman was on a plane to Japan when the news of Kennedy's assassination reached him. He and the other members of the cabinet had the pilots turn around and come back to America. He remembers being very impressed with Johnson's consideration for all the people who were grieving Kennedy's death.

After Republican Richard Nixon gained the White House in the 1968 election, Freeman moved to New York, where he became president of Business International. He worked there to supply information for multinational corporations and to expand trade worldwide.

Eventually, Freeman returned to Washington, D.C., to join the Minnesota-based law firm of Popham and Haik. In 1994 he returned to live in Minnesota.

He and his wife, Jane, have two children, Constance and Michael. Mike continued his father's tradition by becoming a state senator, Hennepin County Attorney, and a candidate for governor of Minnesota.

Freeman has seen government from all angles. He believes that of the governors of Minnesota, the best have been "Floyd B. Olson, the Farmer-Labor governor, who brought great energy and progressive thinking to the governor's office; Harold Stassen, who brought some much-needed reforms; Wendy Anderson, who helped reform our public school system and the financing of our schools; as well as Rudy Perpich for his creativity and enthusiasm and caring for working people."

Orville's advice for school children is, "All of us need to work and study hard, stay in good health and enjoy life to the fullest. We have marvelous public schools today, and we need to make sure that all our school children take advantage of all the options and opportunities, including those in the classrooms and extracurricular activities. We also need to remember to give back to the community we live in, such as helping people in nursing homes, picking up and cleaning the neighborhood and serving in civics clubs and Boy Scouts or Girl Scouts."

Freeman took his governorship very seriously. He said, "The Governor is the Chief Executive of Minnesota. As such, he has a chance to develop policy concerning important areas like education and transportation. He also has a chance to represent the State of Minnesota when new schools and hospitals are dedicated and has an opportunity to represent the State of Minnesota in Washington, D.C., and overseas."

Sources: *Current Biography 1956*, Marjorie Dent Candee, Editor, pp. 192-193. H. W. Wilson Company, New York, 1956; *Minnesota: A History of the State*, by Theodor Blegen, pp. 578-579, University of Minnesota Press, Minneapolis, 1963; interview with Mike Freeman.

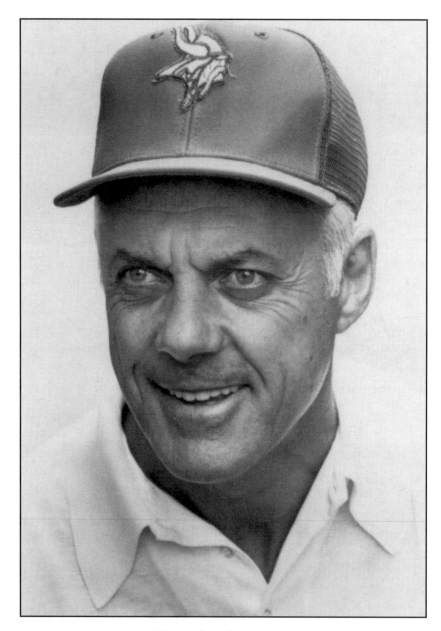

Bud Grant
Pro-Football Coach and Athlete

As an athlete, Bud Grant didn't like to practice, but he was coached by some of the greatest coaching legends in football history. He excelled in three sports in college and played at the top levels of two sports. Yet, he retired from being a professional athlete while still in his prime. He turned to coaching.

Bud Grant grew to be a legend himself. Named Minnesota's greatest athlete for the first half of the Twentieth Century by a panel of sportswriters and sportscasters, Grant became the stoic symbol of the Vikings' glory years.

He was born Harry Peter Grant in Superior, Wisconsin, on May 20, 1927. Nick-named "Bud," he graduated from Superior Central High School, and excelled in sports.

Grant spent a year in the navy at Great Lakes Training Center. There he played football under future NFL coaching great Paul Brown and basketball under Coach Weeb Ewbank, another future NFL coach.

Bud enrolled at the University of Minnesota in 1946. He went on to win nine varsity letters: four in football (twice named All-Big-Ten end), three in basketball, and two in baseball.

His football coach was another legend, Bernie Bierman. It was noted that Bierman's and Grant's intensities were on different levels during practice sessions. But come Saturdays, which were game days, Bud was always ready. He played with grim intensity on both offense and defense.

Also a fine pitcher in baseball, Bud was offered pro contracts in both foot-ball and basketball after college. Grant decided to do both, basketball first.

Bud signed to play in the National Basketball Association with the Minneapolis Lakers in 1949. After two seasons, in which the Lakers won two world championships, Grant signed with the National Football League (NFL) team that had drafted him number one in 1950, the Philadelphia Eagles.

His first year, Grant started as a defensive end. Moved to offense his sec-ond year, Bud caught fifty-two passes to rank second in the NFL, and he was selected to the Pro Bowl that season.

A contract dispute followed and, in 1953, Bud Grant became the first play-er in NFL history to play out his option and become a free agent. He signed to play with the Winnipeg Blue Bombers of the Canadian Football League (CFL).

He starred in the CFL as well, playing offense and defense. He was the Blue Bombers' top pass receiver and starting cornerback. In four CFL seasons, he caught 216 passes and led the league in receptions three times. Bud set a pro football record with five interceptions in one game. He was named a CFL All-Star.

Bud Grant was only twenty-nine when he made another major career decision. This time it was to quit playing and become a coach. For ten years, he coached the Blue Bombers.

His teams ran up a record of 102-56-2. Their playoff record of 20-10-1 resulted in six Western Conference titles and four Grey Cup Championships. Grant was named to the CFL Hall of Fame on May 13, 1983.

But the lure of returning to the NFL persisted for Bud. In 1960, when the new Minnesota Vikings were preparing to enter the league, Bud was offered the head coaching position. Feeling the time was not right, he turned down the offer.

The man who became the Vikings' first coach, Norm Van Brocklin, was let go in 1967. This time Grant accepted the Vikings job and returned to Minnesota.

The team was in disarray. It had won only three games the year before; Van Brocklin had left amid tumultuous controversy; and star quarterback Fran Tarkenton had refused to return to the team.

Bud Grant brought order to the struggling franchise. To veteran Vikings, some of his rules might have seemed extreme. Bud restricted smoking, tightened curfews before games, and even spent time practicing how to line up for the National Anthem.

But there was a method to what some called "Mickey Mouse" rules. Bud wanted to take those forty players from different backgrounds and intellects and make a team out of them. By teaching them to work, train and live together under common rules, Bud hoped to mold them into champions. He didn't have long to wait. His calm, deliberate style and technique would soon reap dividends.

The Vikings won three games and tied three in 1967. The next year Grant and the Vikings won their first Central Division Championship. Ten more Division championships, one NFL and three National Football Conference titles followed. Four times Grant's teams played in the Super Bowl. But the elusive ultimate title, a Super Bowl Championship, was not to be.

Bud retired after the 1983 season. A disastrous 1984 campaign brought him back for one final year. His final 7-9 season restored the Vikings to respectability.

For eighteen years, Bud Grant gazed out at his teams from the Viking sidelines. Minnesota compiled a regular-season record of 158-96-5. Under his tenure, the Vikings made the playoffs twelve times and won fifteen championships.

On January 29, 1994, Bud Grant became the first person elected to both the Canadian and National Football League Halls of Fame when the NFL elected him. Only two coaches have more wins than Grant's 290: George Halas and Don Shula.

Bud never let football consume his life. He loves to hunt and fish. His family is a high priority. In fact, the first time he was named Vikings coach he was late for the announcement because he was fixing a child's bike. When he returned to coach in 1984, he was again late for a press conference; his son's basketball game had run late.

In fact, it was the time commitment that he disliked the most about football. He said, "Having to work seven days, three nights a week for six months, not a day off. Missing time with my family." But the games and the competition were what made it worth if for him. He cannot remember a single game that was the best but says that "after thirty-six years as a pro player or coach and taking part in almost 500 games, it's hard to remember any one. There were many joyous wins and heartbreaking losses."

Bud attributes his stoic appearance on the sidelines during games to the fact that there was not time for emotion. Teams have changed. They are now much bigger and faster, according to Bud. But he still knows how to play his people, for example, if he had to gain one yard he would put in Chuck Foreman, "who would go in, around, or over to get the yard." He also would never tell Fran Tarkenton not to scramble, as Fran made a career of scrambling.

Bud and wife, Pat, divide their time between a home in Bloomington and a lake home in northern Wisconsin. They have six children who all resided in the Twin Cities area.

Bud's advice for school children is, "Take part in as many school activities as you can. You have great opportunities today. Use them!"

Sources: Personal phone interview by author; *True Hearts and Purple Heads*, by Jim Klobuchar, published by Ross and Haines, Minneapolis, 1970.

Jimmy "Jam" Harris and Terry Lewis
Musicians and Producers

It's called the Minneapolis Sound. No one expected that an Upper Midwest city far from the music meccas of both coasts would become a unique and innovative force in popular music.

But then, no one foresaw how a partnership between Jimmy "Jam" Harris and Terry Lewis would develop. Without a snowstorm, it might never have happened.

Jimmy "Jam" was born James Harris III on June 6, 1959, in Minneapolis. He attended Washburn High School. Terry Lewis was born in Omaha, Nebraska, on December 24, 1956. His family soon moved to Minneapolis, where Terry attended North High School, on the side of town opposite from Washburn.

The two met in 1972 at the University of Minnesota. The young men were junior-high students participating in a peer-teaching program called Upward Bound.

Jimmy and Terry both loved music. Despite a difference in music preference, they joined to form their first band, War of Armageddon.

Then the two drifted apart. Jimmy became a very influential club d.j. in Minneapolis, turning songs into hits by rearranging them using a synthesizer and as many as three turntables. His D.J. skills earned him the name Jimmy "Jam."

Terry started a band called Flyte Tyme. Known for its versatility, Terry's band became a standard for Minneapolis music fans.

About this time, Prince Roger Nelson, a high-school friend of Jimmy and Terry's, began to bring the music industry's focus to Minneapolis. Terry persuaded Jimmy to join Flyte Tyme. Then Prince remade the band into the comical and funky sextet, The Time. They signed a deal with Warner Brothers Records in 1981.

In 1982 Jimmy and Terry spent a spring break in Los Angeles as songwriters. Short on cash, they stayed at the home of a friend and subsisted on four-piece chicken dinners from Golden Bird.

The sacrifice was worth it. The young men from Minneapolis made very important contacts that would lead to working with artists like Klymaxx, Reel to Reel, Dynasty, Gladys Knight and the Pips, and the S.O.S. Band.

Then came a snowstorm and a dramatic change in their careers. Jimmy and Terry were touring for The Time's second album. They made a quick trip to Atlanta for an S.O.S. Band session.

But snow delayed their return flight. They missed a concert. An angry Prince fired them both. Later Terry was asked to go back to work with Prince, who was about to do "Purple Rain." When Jimmy encouraged Terry to return to Prince, his friend said, "Forget that! We're in this together."

The two had no written contract between them, just a handshake. They embarked on a career that was to mold a musical style and influence many established and emerging musicians. Prince had taught them a strong work ethic, and with that, they set out to make their mark.

Just after Jimmy and Terry were done working with Prince, the S.O.S. Band's "Just Be Good to Me" became a big hit. Clarence Avant and his Tabu Record label were now convinced that working with Jimmy and Terry would be mutually beneficial.

Avant taught Jam and Lewis about publishing and paired them with singer Cherrelle. The result was a Top 10 hit, "I Didn't Mean to Turn You On."

The duo had begun a dramatic rise to the top level of the music industry as producers. They helped to turn Janet Jackson from one of the "other" Jacksons into a superstar who has sold over forty-million records, including nineteen gold singles, and has seen five albums go multi-platinum.

Boyz II Men earned platinum honors under the tutelage of Jimmy and Terry. The range of recording artists with whom they've worked is awe inspiring, from Robert Palmer to Herb Alpert, Barry White, Rod Stewart, Patti LaBelle, Mariah Carey, Lionel Richie, Michael Jackson, Luther Vandross, TLC, MJB, Vanessa Williams, and many other stars.

Jam and Lewis have written and/or produced nearly one hundred albums and singles that have reached gold, platinum or multi-platinum sales, including twenty-five number-one rhythm-and-blues singles, and twelve number-one pop hits.

But their goal has not been just to just make number-one records. Jimmy and Terry want to give new artists opportunities as well. They also want to support artists of superior quality, even if that means selling fewer records for the sake of artistic freedom. To that end, they created Perspective Records, which has promoted the gospel ensemble Sounds of Blackness, Mint Condition, Solo, and many others.

In 1997, Harris and Lewis started Flyte Tyme Records under the Universal umbrella. They produced the soundtrack for the film, *How Stella Got Her Groove Back*. Once again they melded different music forms, this time with reggae and Caribbean roots, into a compelling sound.

Their success is beyond what two young musicians from Minneapolis probably ever imagined. They are now multimillionaires. The music industry has passed one billion dollars in money generated by their partnership.

Jimmy and Terry have more than fifty gold and platinum plaques. They won their first Grammy in 1986 for Janet Jackson's *Control*. Janet also won for "That's The Way Love Goes" in 1993 for Best R&B Song. Her song "Again" was nominated for an Academy Award and Golden Globe.

They have received the NAACP Image Award and ASCAP's Writers of the Year honors, a Grammy for Producers of the Year, and have earned Billboard awards. Jimmy and Terry have a star on the Hollywood Walk of Fame.

Jimmy and his wife, Lisa, have three children. Terry is divorced and has three children.

It's been twenty-seven years since it all began for Jimmy and Terry. The trust established at the beginning continues. They split everything down the middle, fifty-fifty.

They still look ahead. Whether working with established stars, developing new ones or branching into the sounds of motion pictures, Terry and Jimmy continue to mold the sound for listeners, nationally and internationally.

From their background in Minneapolis, listening to the Carpenters, Chicago, Kool and the Gang, and Earth, Wind, and Fire, they have achieved greater success than they could have imagined. Terry said, "We don't measure success by finances or the number of hits we've had. Success is the sense of accomplishment one gets from doing what they set out to do. All of those things come to pass through respect."

The secret to their success is to "get the artist involved in the creative process. That way their feelings and thoughts go into the songs." Jimmy's and Terry's advice to school children is, "Education is the key."

Source: Susan Blond, Inc. biographical material provided by Flyte Tyme.

Nellie Stone Johnson

Activist

She faced harsh prejudice and discrimination, not just because of her color, but because she was a young, aggressive woman from rural Minnesota attempting to succeed in the early twentieth century.

But Nellie Stone Johnson persevered. In the words of State Representative Steve Wenzel, "She won the respect and admiration of Minnesota's highest political leaders. Nellie was a confidant of Hubert Humphrey, a truly remarkable woman."

Nellie rose from humble beginnings to walk with the giants of Minnesota politics and government.

She was born Nellie Allen on December 17, 1905, in Lakeville, Minnesota. Her father, William Allen, wanted to be a dairy farmer, and the family ended up moving northward to Hinckley, Minnesota.

Education formed a solid foundation for Nellie's family. Her father was a member of the school board in Dakota County. Her mother and grandmother were teachers.

Nellie attended school in Hinckley but left before graduation. In that era, it was not uncommon for girls, especially in rural Minnesota, to do so.

But Nellie had a thirst for knowledge that would not be quenched. She learned wherever and whenever she could. She moved from home at seventeen years of age to finish high school through a GED program at the University of Minnesota.

She entered the labor force, working at the Minneapolis Athletic Club as a hat-check girl, then as an elevator operator and starter, and finally as a receptionist at the club.

Through all that, she still made time to pursue knowledge. Nellie continued to study at the University of Wisconsin. "Wisconsin had the best labor and agricultural studies in the United States," she related.

She financed her education in Wisconsin through money she earned from trapping. During the depression of the 1930s, Nellie continued to study. "I did a smattering of a lot of schools. They were reaching out for labor people," she explained. "It wasn't a formal kind of education, but you got the knowledge anyway."

Northwestern and the University of Chicago were among the schools where Nellie studied. "I learned whatever I could," she said. "I was kind of a hound dog for studying everything that came along. I had a haphazard education, but I learned a lot from it."

It wasn't easy to be a black woman seeking higher education. "There were a lot of clichés about anybody that was black, whether you were a man or woman. You felt it coming through the air. I certainly felt it at the University of Minnesota," Stone Johnson said.

"When I first stuck my head in the agricultural door, it hit me like a bombshell. It felt like they were thinking, 'Where in the world did this pig come from that calls herself a farmer?'

"The looks you got just told you. Of course, I've had that down through the years in other things that I've tried to do."

Nellie worked for the Minneapolis Athletic Club until 1949. Then she opened a small sewing alteration shop, which she operated for thirty-four years. As she worked to support herself, Nellie's real passion became public service and the labor movement.

She started organizing labor unions in 1934. She became the first female president of Local 665 Hotel and Restaurant Employees Union. She was involved in labor and politics throughout the 1930s and 1940s.

Nellie's political interest was natural. Her father was a member of the progressive Non-Partisan League, and he later became a member of Minnesota's Farmer-Labor Party.

One of Stone Johnson's first forays into party politics was in the gubernatorial campaign of Floyd B. Olson.

"He was a truly humane person," Nellie recalled. "Governor Olson was close to labor and to farmers."

Olson, elected in 1930, died prior to his 1936 re-election campaign. "I think President [Franklin D.] Roosevelt had plans for Governor Olson to become the next president," Nellie stated.

She also advised a rising young politician in Minneapolis. His name was Hubert H. Humphrey.

"He was a South Dakota man. What did he know about race? So I tried to tell him the way it looked to me. We came together pretty good," she recalled.

"At the same time, we talked about forming a new political party. I talked to Hubert about equality for people and how important that was. I think that concern for race relations rubbed off on him and carried over to help women as well. He seemed to take more interest in equality for women after we had a lot of talks."

In the 1940s, Nellie was part of the merger committee that brought about the unification of the Farmer-Labor and Democrat Parties in Minnesota. Thus, she, along with Humphrey, became one of the founders of the DFL Party.

Stone Johnson's commitment to education and public service was far reaching. She served on the Higher Education Board and on the Minnesota State University Board for eight years. She served on the Minnesota State Colleges and Universities Board of Trustees as well. She was the first black person elected to city-wide office when she won a seat on the library board in 1946.

Stone Johnson maintained her lifelong commitment to race relations and women through membership in the National Council of Negro Women, the National Coalition of Labor Women, and the National League of Women Voters. A life member of the National Association for the Advancement of Colored People, Nellie served on its board for twenty-six years. She worked on behalf of her own community as a member of the Minneapolis Urban League.

Twice in her life Nellie married, first to Clyde Stone and then to Percy Lee Johnson. Both unions ended in divorce. She continues to make her home in Minneapolis.

Many honors have been bestowed on Nellie for her service. Among them is the Cecil E. Newman Humanitarian Award. In 1995, she and a longtime political friend, former Vice-President Walter Mondale, were awarded honorary doctorate degrees from St. Cloud State University.

Representative Wenzel called Nellie, "An amazing woman. She's been a pioneer in Minnesota's progressive movement. She's been out front in race relations, women's rights, education, and labor causes."

Nellie's advice to today's youth is simple. "Treat everybody right as a human being."

Source: Minnesota-State-University-provided biography. Interview with Ms. Stone Johnson.

Linda Kelsey

Actor

The pretty, young, red-haired newspaper reporter earnestly pleaded the case for her story to her hard-bitten, crusty editor. Her passion and commitment to the cause she was pitching were plainly evident.

For many, this is the image of Linda Kelsey that endures. For five years, she played reporter Billie Newman in the highly acclaimed CBS television series *Lou Grant*.

But TV work was not all fun and games. "I would get to the studio at about 6:30 in the morning for make-up, we would start filming about 8:00 a.m., and I'd go home about 8:00 p.m., learn my lines for the next day, and start all over! Most of the time we were on a set at the studio, but sometimes we would be at a location somewhere in Los Angeles, particularly if we were shooting an outdoors shot."

The long-running show allowed the creative process to develop the characters, but the long hours made it hard to keep a social life.

Kelsey was born in Minneapolis, Minnesota, on July 28, 1946. She grew up in St. Paul and attended Washington High School before going on to the University of Minnesota.

Drama appealed to Kelsey since she was a young girl. Her childhood amusements involved putting on plays for the neighborhood children. Linda took part in school acting and many other high-school activities.

At the University of Minnesota, Kelsey received a McKnight Fellowship in acting. She began her professional career at the famed Guthrie Theatre, where she appeared for two seasons in roles such as Miranda in *The Tempest*, Maggie in *The Lovers*, and Teresa in *The Hostage*.

After college, Linda moved to Los Angeles, where greater acting opportunities were available. Her theatrical appearances flourished as she worked with prominent figures. John Lithgow directed her in the role of Creena in *A Pagan Place* at the Long Wharf Theater. She appeared with Charlton Heston at the Ahmanson, portraying Mary Warren in Alfred Miller's *The Crucible*.

Kelsey played Nellie in the Eva Marie Saint production of *Summer and Smoke* at the Kennedy Center. She co-starred in the West Coast premiere of *Duet for One* at the Back Alley Theater. And she appeared in the feature film *Midnight Man* with Burt Lancaster.

But it is her television roles, especially in *Lou Grant*, that offer the most enduring image of Linda Kelsey. She was Billie Newman from 1978 to 1983. During those five years, she received five Emmy nominations for her portrayals.

In addition to her success on *Lou Grant*, Kelsey has amassed an impressive list of television credits. She had guest starring roles on more than thirty television series, including *Touched by an Angel, E.R., The Mary Tyler Moore Show, M*A*S*H*, The Twilight Zone, Streets of San Francisco, St. Elsewhere, Ray Bradbury Theater*, and *Midnight Caller*.

Linda starred in made-for-television movies including *A Perfect Match, Something for Joey, A Family Torn Apart, If Someone Had Known*, and *A Place to Be*.

In the miniseries *Eleanor and Franklin*, Linda played the role of Lucy Murcer. She appeared as Lee Remick's sister in *Nutcracker: Money, Madness and Mayhem*.

Kelsey made two other forays into series television, as Kate Harper on *Day by Day* for NBC and, more recently, as Carol on the Billie Crystal HBO series, *Sessions*.

Linda's return to Minnesota was the result of a business opportunity for her husband. In the Twin Cities, she has continued to perform and contribute to Minnesota's vibrant theater scene. At the Park Square Theater in St. Paul, she appeared as Constance in *Good Night, Desdemona*. She has also played Dorthea in *Eleemosynary* at the Park Square Theater.

Linda and her husband have two teenage daughters. In addition to her acting, she has served as the arts correspondent for WCCO-TV.

Linda's advice for school children is: "I think some kids think that success happens almost magically, that a person is 'discovered,' and that's all there is to it. I advise kids, whatever their interests, to really study and learn all they can. It's really a great thing to try to achieve mastery at something. Acting is no exception. The actors I know who are really great, never stop growing and exploring their art. Also, I would like to encourage kids to think less about what kind of money they will make at something and more about what they can contribute back to the world with their own talents and gifts."

Source: Biographical material provided by subject.

Harmon Killebrew
Pro-Baseball Hall of Famer

They called him the "Killer." Every time he dug in at the plate, the Minnesota Twins' crowds at Metropolitan Stadium were rife with anticipation. Maybe this time Harmon would rocket another moonshot high and deep over the left-field fence.

Fans watched as, after a monumental swing, he stood at the plate and admire the flight of the ball as if he were an artist applying the final stroke to a painting.

He was Harmon Killebrew; 573 times he circled the bases with home runs. He played fourteen years with the Minnesota Twins. For most of those years, his name was synonymous with baseball in Minnesota.

Born June 29, 1936, in Payette, Idaho, Harmon loved baseball from childhood. One of his favorite memories of youth concerns baseball. He related the story at his hall of fame induction ceremony in Cooperstown. Killebrew strongly believes that baseball shapes character, as his father before him.

His father was a great proponent of his playing baseball. "We were playing baseball as a child in our front yard. We were making holes in the grass for bases. My mother commented to my father that we should probably stop playing ball in the front yard as the grass was really getting ruined. My dad said, 'We are not raising grass, we are raising boys!'"

Harmon wanted to play baseball from second grade. Many young boys can only dream to follow Killebrew's progression. He started playing when he was seven, then advanced to high-school ball. While playing semi-pro ball, he was spotted by Washington Senators' farm director Ossie Bluege after Idaho Senator Herman Welker recommended that the scout take a look at Harmon.

Harmon's power came naturally. His father, Clay, was a great college football fullback. His grandfather, Culver Killebrew, was reputed to be the heavyweight champion of the Illinois detachment of the Union army in the Civil War. Harmon was fortunate to have strength in his family, for in those days weights and strength training were discouraged. It was feared that baseball players would get too muscle-bound.

Killebrew signed with the Senators at the age of seventeen. For two years, he languished on the bench of the major-league team. Then, for the next three seasons, he divided his time between short stays with the Senators and the rest of the time with minor-league teams in Charlotte, Chattanooga, and Indianapolis.

In 1959, Senators' owner Calvin Griffith called his manager Cookie Lavagetto aside and told him it was time to play the young man from Idaho full-time. Harmon immediately rewarded Griffith's confidence. In his breakthrough year of 1959, he hit .242 with forty-two home runs (tying a club record) and 105 runs batted in.

It was the beginning of a remarkable run. After one more year in Washington, the team moved westward and became the Minnesota Twins.

There Killebrew would go on to win five home-run titles, leading the league in RBIs three times and in slugging percentages twice.

In 1960 he became the first player in twenty-five years to hit a homer onto the left-field roof at Tiger Stadium in Detroit. Two years later Harmon topped that by rocketing one completely over the Detroit left-field roof. He came just short of putting one out of Memorial Stadium in Baltimore.

At Metropolitan Stadium in Bloomington, the Twins' original Minnesota home, Killebrew shot one a distance of 462 feet and fifteen feet up the green batter's eye in center field. On July 4, 1961, Harmon—never known as a speedster—hit the first inside-the-park home run in Met Stadium history after Chicago outfielder Jim Landis collided with the center-field fence in a futile attempt to catch Killebrew's blast.

Harmon's most monumental home run came at Metropolitan Stadium, when he lofted one high into the second deck, 521 feet from home plate. The spot is commemorated with a plaque in the Mall of America, which was built where Met Stadium was.

Eight times Killebrew hit over forty home runs in a season. Ten times he cracked over thirty homers, and nine times Harmon drove in over one hundred runs. In 1969 he was named the American League's Most Valuable Player when he hit forty-nine home runs, drove in 140 runs, and walked 145 times to lead the league in all categories.

The Twins prospered from the "Killer's" prowess. In 1965 they won the American League title, but lost in seven games to the Dodgers in Harmon's only World Series. Killebrew hit .286 in the World Series and launched a home run off ace Don Drysdale.

In 1969 and 1970, the Twins won the American League West Championship, but went on to lose the American League Championship Series to the Baltimore Orioles.

Sadly, Killebrew played his last year in Kansas City after the Twins released him following the 1974 season. But his legendary career is forever part of Twins' history. He hit 573 home runs, fifth all-time in major-league baseball and second only to Babe Ruth in the American League.

Killebrew holds team records for home runs, runs batted in, and walks. Harmon's jersey number 3 was retired by the Twins in a ceremony on August 11, 1974. He became the first Twin elected to the Baseball Hall of Fame on January 10, 1984.

After his playing career ended, Killebrew returned to Idaho where he joined a former congressman in an insurance business, Killebrew & Harding, Inc. From 1976 to 1984, Harmon worked with his partner selling business insurance and estate planning.

The business expanded in 1979 when E.F. Hutton Financial Services joined forces with Killebrew and Harding. They opened an office in Boise, Idaho, and made Harmon vice-president of operations. Adding a third partner in 1984, the company became Killebrew, Harper, & Harper.

In 1987 Harmon left the insurance business to devote time to his automobile dealership, Harmon Killebrew Motors, begun in 1984 in Ontario, Oregon.

He sold the dealership in 1990 and moved to Scottsdale, Arizona, where he established his current business, Professional Endorsements.

In addition to his business pursuits, Killebrew did some special assignment coaching for the Twins and worked as a Twins television broadcaster, as well as brief stints broadcasting Oakland A's and California Angels games.

He and his wife, Nita, have five children and nine grandchildren.

In retirement, Harmon smashes golf balls near his Arizona home instead of baseballs out of American League parks. But he still thinks that baseball is the greatest game ever developed and that it has not changed. However, he does think that the history of the game should be emphasized more. For Harmon, the greatest player to ever play pro ball is Babe Ruth, and the best pitcher is Whitey Ford. Harmon's favorite memory from his career is "every day I walked on the field."

He did not try to be a role model, but is pleased that he provided a good image for kids. His advice for school children is, "Stay in school. Do the best you can. Get an education and go as far as you can."

Source: Minnesota Twins provided biography, *2000 Twins Media Guide*, author interview.

Mike Kingery
Professional Baseball Player

Mike Kingery was in very familiar surroundings when he, outfielder for the Pittsburgh Pirates, was announced as a pinch hitter in a game at Coors Field in Denver. Mike had played for the Colorado Rockies the previous two years.

Now a Pirate, he was mired in a slump. Pittsburgh fans had booed him. For the first time in his career as a professional baseball player, Mike felt that his home team fans did not appreciate his efforts. And here, in his former home stadium, he was being put in to pinch hit in front of his old home crowd when his new team was hopelessly behind.

But, while standing in the on-deck circle, he could feel the Rockies' fans begin to call his name and cheer. As he strode to the plate to hit, the throng rose in a lusty cheer of welcome.

Mike responded by slapping a base hit. When he reached first base, the Rockies' first sacker Andres Gallaraga smiled at Kingery and said, "I knew Kingery would get a hit, Kingery is a pro."

As he proceeded around the bases that inning, other Rockies players called their encouragement to him, including Dante Bischette, who shouted greetings from left field.

Those who know Mike Kingery do appreciate and respect his skills as a ball player and a person. The road to Denver that day had been a long and bumpy one for the man from Atwater, Minnesota. But he had persevered and persisted and lasted seventeen years in pro baseball.

Mike was born in St. James, Minnesota, on March 29, 1961, the youngest of four brothers. His parents, Ken and Marion Kingery, moved the family to Atwater when Mike was a youngster. There they had purchased the local bowling alley.

Mike was raised in Atwater, where he was a star athlete in football, basketball, track, and baseball. He graduated from Atwater High School in 1979.

A big break for Mike came when his local team qualified for the State Legion Baseball Tournament the summer following graduation. There professional scouts got a look at the Atwater youth. In September of 1979, Mike signed his first professional contract with the Kansas City Royals of the American Baseball League.

Thus began a journey that would see Mike play for fourteen different teams, including six major-league clubs. He and his wife, Christy, whom he married in 1982, would move fifty-four times in fifteen years.

For the 1980 season, Mike reported to Sarasota, Kansas City's club in the Florida Rookie League. It took until mid-season in 1986 and stints with minor-league teams in Charleston, Ft. Meyers, Memphis, and Omaha before he got the call to report to the Royals.

But also joining the Royals was a superstar athlete named Bo Jackson. It became a case of too many outfielders, and the Royals sent Mike to the Seattle Mariners after the 1986 season.

Kingery's first full major-league season was 1987 with the Mariners. He batted .280. For the next six years, Mike bounced between several minor- and major-league teams, including big-league time with the San Francisco Giants and Oakland A's.

In 1994 he caught on with the Colorado Rockies and enjoyed his most productive time in the "bigs." In the strike-shortened season, he batted .349 and was named Rockie of the Month for July.

Kingery was even honored with a moniker from Chris Berman of ESPN's Baseball Tonight. The commentator dubbed him, "Mike, the Man Who Would Be Kingery."

The year 1995 was another satisfying year for Mike, for the Rockies made the playoffs as a wild-card team. But the reality of being a professional athlete is that there is little security, especially for a good, solid player who's not a superstar, the category into which Kingery fell. After the 1995 campaign, the Rockies released Mike.

In 1996, he caught on for one final season with the Pittsburgh Pirates. Following a slow start, he picked up his hitting after the series against Denver. Kingery hoped to return to Pittsburgh the following year.

However, on Christmas Eve of 1996, he received word that the Pirates would not offer him a contract again. Mike and Christy decided it was time to retire. The days of travel and uncertainty were over.

Deeply religious, Mike decided to devote his time to his family, teaching and coaching. For years, Christy and Mike had home-schooled their daughters. Now Mike could devote more time to their education.

They made Atwater their home. Mike began a career in speaking to youth and church groups, as well as providing baseball instruction to teams and individual young athletes. He founded Solid Foundation Baseball School and began to conduct baseball camps as well.

In 1999 the couple constructed a new home near Grove City, a town neighboring Atwater. Their family included seven children: daughters, Rachel, Anna, Michelle, Rebekah, Elizabeth, and Abigail, and son, David.

Mike's advice for school children is, "Realize that you were created by the hand of a loving God. You are very special to Him. He has a special plan and purpose for your life, which includes to know Him personally. Respect and obey your authorities and seek to be a positive role model for those around you."

One of Mike's favorite memories is of Mike Kingery Day with the Twins. "In September of my first year in the major leagues, while playing for the Kansas City Royals, I made my first trip home to play against the Minnesota Twins. The city of Atwater and the Twins sponsored a Mike Kingery Day. Kent Hrbek presented my wife, Christy, with a bouquet of flowers at home plate. I spoke to the crowd (about twenty percent of the 5,000 in attendance were there to see me play.) Mr. Phil Trooien, my high-school baseball coach, threw out the first pitch—which I caught. The choir from my home church, Evangelical Free Church, sang the National Anthem. I got four hits that night. What an exciting night! George Brett told me that he still has his Mike Kingery Day button."

Of all the teams on which he played, Colorado was his favorite. The fans were great, and he was in the line-up every day.

Mike looked up to his brother as a child. "He always dragged me along with him, even though I was eleven years his junior. I was the bat boy for his softball and baseball teams. He was a tremendous athlete, playing three sports in college and bowling numerous 300s—including one at age thirteen."

Source: Biographical material provided by subject; personal interview by author.

Jonny Lang
Musician

Jonny Lang has made his home in Minnesota since his early teens, when he began a recording career that made him a Grammy Awards nominee before age twenty.

Jonny was born into a musically talented family in Fargo, North Dakota, on January 29, 1981. His own interest in music was cultivated during his early years on the family's Castleton farm, near Fargo. Jonny's parents brought him to listen to bands that performed in the region. With his mother, an excellent singer, and his father, a drummer in a country-music band, Jonny and his three sisters, two older and one younger, naturally acquired a love for music.

Jonny has said that he "just always knew" he'd be a singer. His family was big into blues, rhythm and blues, and Motown music. Jonny listened and even tried to mimic singers during his early childhood. He never quite mastered Michael Jackson's "Moon Walk," however.

The aspiring star made a fortuitous contact when he went to his first concert at age twelve. A local band, Bad Medicine, was performing blues music. Afterward, Jonny talked to the lead guitarist of the group, Ted Larsen, and asked him for guitar lessons.

Larsen told Jonny, "I'm gonna teach you blues, or I'm not gonna teach you," which was fine with Jonny, whose favorite musicians included B.B. King, Stevie Wonder, and James Taylor.

Thus began the launching of a legend. Jonny practiced every day, all day. His family began to homeschool him so that he could devote more time to his music. Jonny enjoyed studying science as well as music. In a year, he joined Ted Larsen's band as lead singer. They became Kid Jonny and the Big Bang, making hundreds of appearances in the Dakotas and Minnesota.

Within two years, Jonny and his family moved to Minneapolis, Minnesota, where he began his recording career and now makes his home.

His independent release, *Smokin'*, sold over 25,000 copies and led to Lang's signing with a major record label, A&M.

In 1997, Jonny debuted *Lie to Me*. His singing and guitar playing on the title song rocketed him to the top of the new artist album charts. He performed on national TV shows.

Greats in the blues field, men who were Jonny's idols, began to recognize young Lang as a significant talent. Soon he found himself playing alongside such blues giants as Luther Allison, Lonnie Brooks, and Buddy Guy.

A highlight for the young artist came when the legendary B.B King asked Jonny onstage to sing with him. Lang said, "We toured together for a month and he invited me up on stage to jam. We had a blast. I'd look over at him and realize that I was sitting next to God."

In the *Los Angeles Times*, King commented about his young friend, "Jonny Lang's sixteen, so he's got youth and talent with it. When I was young, I didn't play like I do today. So these kids are starting at the height that I've reached. Think what they might do over time."

After the release of *Lie to Me*, Jonny went on the road touring with King, Aerosmith, The Rolling Stones, and Blues Traveler. As his fame blossomed, he evolved into a headline performer. He developed a professional relationship with David Z, who wrote songs with Jonny and produced *Wander This World*. The latter work earned Lang a 1999 Grammy nomination for Best Contemporary Blues Album.

In his newer releases, Jonny expanded from blues to R&B, rock, and ballads. Lang said he plans to continue to stretch his work into funk, soul, and R&B.

Lang plays down the glitz that marks many young performers in favor of a more traditional approach. He plays to his song. He even includes his mother and sister in performances, giving a "family" atmosphere to his show.

Jonny Lang, at his young age, is a phenomenal talent. Yet, he is just beginning to touch the potential that lies ahead. As the late Luther Allison said, "Jonny Lang has the power to move the music into the next millennium by reaching the ears of a new generation. The great musicians have the power to break all of the 'isms'-race, age, sex. . . . Jonny Lang is one of those musicians."

When asked how long it took for him to learn to play guitar, Jonny replied, "I'm still learning."

Jonny's advice to school children is "make lots of good friends. Oh! And study real hard, and listen to your moms and dads and teachers. P.S. And buy my CDs."

Source: A & M Records Website.

Tom Lehman
Professional Golfer

It would have been easy for Tom Lehman to quit. As 1986 dawned, both his
professional golfing and his personal life were at low ebb. For three years in a row, he had failed to qualify for the major Professional Golf Association (PGA) Tour. He had made little money in golf, while friends with whom he'd attended college and tour school had gone on to big wins and big earnings. And then his girlfriend, Melissa, left him.

A man low on both self-esteem and self-confidence, Tom thought of turning to other pursuits. But Lehman didn't quit the sport he loved. Instead, he showed the perseverance and dedication that would make him a champion.

Born in Austin, Minnesota, on March 7, 1959, Lehman was raised in the central Minnesota town of Alexandria. He used to shag golf balls for his father with his baseball glove. He loved hockey, but couldn't skate, so he played basketball, football, and golf in high school. He first played golf at age seven.

He was successful in varsity golf but not enough to draw notice from college recruiters. Tom decided to get on with his life by going to St. John's University near St. Cloud, Minnesota. He planned to go into business after earning his degree.

Just two days before he was to start classes at St. John's, Lehman's path took an unexpected hook. He received a phone call from the University of Minnesota's golf coach, who wanted to know whether the young man would like to play golf for him. Quickly accepting the chance to earn a spot with the Gophers, Tom was at the university when classes started there two weeks later.

It proved a good match for both the athlete and the school. Lehman spent four years with the Gopher links team and was named All-American for three seasons. Tom notes, that although Minnesota's climate allows for a break from the game to follow other pursuits, it does limit the amount of practice and repetition a player can get.

After his college success, Tom's goal was to earn his card and qualify for the PGA Tour. In 1982, he attended tour school and realized his dream. He was ready to earn his fortune in professional golf.

But sometimes dreams lead to nightmares. Tom Lehman wouldn't win a PGA tour event until more than a decade later in 1994. He wouldn't win a major tournament for fourteen years. The intervening years were marred by enormous frustrations: months on the road playing small tournaments for little or no money; failing to make cuts; having little or no personal life.

It was early in his golf career, in 1984, that Tom met Melissa. By late 1985, his confidence was at an all-time low as his professional and personal lives went sour. He couldn't regain his playing card; his money was about gone; and the pressures of maintaining a long-distance relationship were too much. Melissa said she didn't want to see him again.

Mulling over his problems, the golfer from Minnesota decided it was time to make major changes in his life. Tom decided to quit the tour in favor of a more stable lifestyle. He accepted the position of golf pro for the Wood Ranch Golf Club. He and Melissa began to talk again. A normal lifestyle led to tranquility and nurtured their relationship. On June 27, 1987, Tom and Melissa were married.

That year Lehman played in just one tournament, the U.S. Open. He missed the cut by only one shot and played well enough to become confident and enthused about golf again.

Tom and his bride decided to give his dreams of playing professional golf one more try. Tom went to South Africa to play. Next he played in Asia and in mini-tours in smaller cities across the United States.

Then another turning point came. Lehman decided that money wasn't the sole motivating factor in his game. He really wanted to be good. That meant returning to tour school. Once again, Tom was trying to qualify to get his card back. He started out poorly, but his caddy, Deli Logan, continued to offer encouragement.

"You're a champion, you got to play like a champion!" Deli Logan cried.

Lehman did. After a disastrous seventy-eight on the first round, he burned up the course the next three days—only to fall one stroke short of getting his card back.

He was crushed and, a religious man, doubted God's role for him as much as he doubted himself. Then he considered that maybe God had a better plan. Playing on the Hogan Tour instead of the regular PGA Tour, Lehman was able to develop the newfound confidence that he had gained those last three rounds at tour school.

But Lehman won more than self-belief. He was named the Hogan Tour's Player of the Year. For the first time he made decent money. More important, that honor gave Lehman the number-one exempt spot on the PGA Tour for the following year. He had finally earned his second chance. He was determined to make the most of it.

In 1992, Tom Lehman finished twenty-fourth in the PGA Tour. The next year he was third in the Masters. In 1994, on the final day of the Masters Tournament, he had the lead, but Jose Marieolathalo came from behind to beat him.

Lehman recalled, "At that point I was so disappointed. On the one hand, I had lost the Masters; but on the other hand, I didn't fold up under the pressure. I had handled myself pretty well under the heat. Second wasn't all bad, so I felt pretty good about that."

On the heels of his fine 1994 Masters showing, Lehman tasted his first PGA win, which came at Memorial. But he faced disappointment in the 1995 Masters, where he was bothered by health problems and finished fortieth. After a checkup revealed nothing serious, Lehman regained his focus and won his second tournament at Colonial. Next came the 1995 Ryder Cup series, where he developed special memories and friendships to last a lifetime.

The year 1996 started frustratingly for Tom. He was playing well but just couldn't win. He finished third in Hawaii. He lost by two in Los Angeles. He was thwarted at the U.S. Open, too; if Lehman had landed his drive off the eighteenth tee onto the fairway, he probably would have won the Open. Instead, his drive went through the fairway and into a bunker. Tom was earning a reputation for not being able to win "the big one."

Next came the 1996 British Open. Trying to hold off the charge of Nick Faldo, Lehman had a two-stroke lead as he approached the eighteenth green. He told himself, "Tom, if you can keep yourself out of the bunker on your second shot, out of the crowd on the green somewhere, you can win this thing."

Tom hit a good drive down the rough and stayed out of the bunker. It was about 185 yards to the hole. He made the green with an eight iron and two putted. Tom Lehman, the boy from rural Minnesota, was a major tournament champion! He was 1996 Player of the Year and leading money winner with $1,780,159, a record at that time.

Lehman closed out the year with a tremendous performance in the Tour Championship. He won by six strokes and pocketed $540,000.

The Minnesota golfer achieved no major wins in 1997, but he came very close twice. He lost a playoff at the Mercedes Championship to Tiger Woods. In the U.S. Open, he fell to Ernie Els by two strokes.

Tom rang in 1998 with his most prosperous victory ever. He won a $1,000,000 prize at the Williams World Challenge on January 2. Then, at the end of the month, Tom followed up by winning just over $500,000 by finishing atop the leader board in the Phoenix Open.

As with most athletes, Lehman has had ups and downs since that great win. On the down side, he pulled a muscle before a tournament while playing with his kids. He had colon surgery that cost him a month of play.

But, after years of perseverance, success has become a more frequent companion for Lehman. He was on Ryder Cup teams in 1995, 1997, and 1999. He played on the President's Cup team in 1994 and 1995. He scored major wins to shake off the reputation of not being able to win "the big one."

The Minnesotan is quick to credit his marriage with giving him focus to do well on the tour. Also, he is eager to give back. Tom is host of the Dayton's Challenge, an annual charity event in Minneapolis that raises money for the Children's Cancer Research Fund. He also spends much time with his family and church.

He emphasizes his own values over the glamour and riches of the pro circuit. When asked what his most thrilling moment in golf has been, Tom Lehman doesn't talk about the fame and big money that come from big victories. He talks about playing for his country and its dramatic come-from-behind victory in the 1999 Ryder Cup.

Lehman's favorite golf course is Shinnecock Hills, and his favorite golfer is Arnold Palmer.

Lehman advises, "Consider where your priorities are, where your faith is," to keep perspective and gain the strength needed to persevere against life's challenges. "Don't forget to have fun."

Source: Life Story Foundation: Tom Lehman (Website); www.pgatour.com.

Eugene McCarthy
United States Senator

In 1968, Eugene McCarthy brought down a president of the United States and changed American foreign policy. His actions helped to end one war and just may have prevented future wars from happening. He started life as a small-town boy in Watkins, Minnesota, but McCarthy grew into a powerful figure whose actions carried worldwide impact.

As a youth, McCarthy liked to play baseball. He looked up to Adlai Stevenson, seeing him as someone who could bring about change. He considered dedicating his life to serving others and had early thoughts of becoming a priest. Instead, commitment to his values led him to decades of serving others in the public sector.

Gene McCarthy was born in Watkins in 1916. He attended college at nearby St. John's University in Collegeville, Minnesota, and then at the University of Minnesota, where he earned a master of arts degree.

McCarthy first used that education to be a teacher. He taught English at a public high school and economics at St. John's. He took a hiatus to serve as a civilian technical assistant for military intelligence during World War II, from 1942 to 1946.

After the war, McCarthy resumed teaching, this time at the University of St. Thomas. His classes in sociology and economics were filled with young men back from the war. He taught a social problems and issues class that was particularly relevant to the problems they faced in the post-war world.

Gene married Abigail Quigley in 1945. They had met while both were teaching high school in Mandan, North Dakota, in the early 1940s. Gene and Abigail would have two daughters and one son.

In 1948, Gene McCarthy decided to put his classroom theories into practice, realizing that in teaching about social problems, he was dealing with the problems of the day. He ran as a Democrat for the House of Representatives in Minnesota's Fourth Congressional District, comprised mostly of St. Paul. The Watkins native was soon a congressman.

U.S. Rep. McCarthy was quick to make his mark. He was a founder of the Democratic Study Group, first called "McCarthy's Mavericks." He debated the fanatical United States senator from Wisconsin, Joseph McCarthy, in 1952. Congressman Gene McCarthy from Minnesota was one of the few people willing to fight the persecuting witch hunts for Communists launched by Senator Joe McCarthy.

After serving fro one-decade in the House, Eugene was elected to the United States Senate from Minnesota in 1958. Re-elected in 1964, he served on the Senate's Finance and Foreign Relations committees.

McCarthy's national prominence grew in 1964, when President Lyndon Johnson let it be known that he was considering both of Minnesota's Democratic senators, McCarthy and Hubert H. Humphrey, for the vice presidency.

Milking the press and public to build interest in the nominating convention, Johnson kept everyone guessing who his pick would be until nearly the last moment. Then he announced his choice of Humphrey.

Many years later, McCarthy said that he simply wouldn't make all the commitments to Johnson that were asked of him, while Humphrey did. Vietnam was not yet an issue and did not come up in discussions because Johnson was on record against expanding war in Southeast Asia.

The Johnson-Humphrey team went on to defeat the Republican ticket, Arizona Governor Barry Goldwater and Rep. William Miller of New York. Soon afterward, Johnson drastically escalated the war in Vietnam. By 1966, Sen. Gene McCarthy was speaking out against the war.

In his 1967 book, *The Limits of Power*, Senator McCarthy said of that war, "Three points must be raised about our involvement in Vietnam. First, assuming that we understand what we mean by victory, is there a possibility of victory? Second, what would be the cost of that victory? Third, what assurance do we have that a better world or a better society will emerge in Vietnam following that victory?

"The answers should be positive on each of these three counts. I do not believe that they are positive."

A dramatic split grew between McCarthy and Johnson over the Vietnam War, leading to the senator's challenge of his president in the New Hampshire Democratic presidential primary election of 1968.

The New Hampshire primary became a referendum on Johnson's policy in Vietnam. College students and others opposed to the war got "clean for Gene" as they trudged through the snows of the Northeast campaigning for McCarthy.

The New Hampshire primary results stunned the nation and the president. Eugene McCarthy garnered forty-two percent of the vote to Johnson's forty-nine percent. With 211 delegates, the senator from Minnesota actually had totaled more than President Johnson.

Although LBJ had technically won the primary vote in New Hampshire, the reality was that he had been given a vote of no-confidence in his policies. Three weeks later he dropped out of the race, announcing that he would not be a candidate for re-election.

Gene McCarthy had lost one competitor, but he quickly picked up two others. New York Senator Bobby Kennedy and Vice-President Hubert Humphrey soon entered the race.

McCarthy courageously pressed on. America was in turmoil. Protests against the war mounted on college campuses and elsewhere. Racial tensions continued to build, exploding into riots with the assassination of Dr. Martin Luther King, Jr.

Then McCarthy defeated Senator Kennedy in the Oregon primary. That same night the New York senator won in California, only to be tragically assassinated as he left a hotel.

That left the two Minnesotans, McCarthy and Humphrey, to battle on to Chicago for the Democratic nomination. Chicago was a disaster for McCarthy and his supporters. Since Mayor Richard Daley backed Humphrey, the Chicago police force had little sympathy for McCarthy's supporters.

The National Democratic Convention of 1968 generated major headlines out of Chicago as violence erupted. Amidst the mayhem, some McCarthy supporters were targets of tear gas and police beatings. The convention ended with Gene's defeat by Humphrey. It left the Democratic Party sharply divided. Humphrey was tied to President Johnson's Vietnam policy because of his association with the administration.

Although he tried to distance himself from Johnson, the disastrous convention and taint of the war were too much to overcome. In a narrow victory, Republican former Vice-President Richard Nixon was elected president. Gradually, Nixon changed policy and slowly brought an end to war in Vietnam, unlike *Gene*, who would have stopped military action immediately.

Eugene McCarthy left the Senate in 1970 to return to his role as educator. He taught university courses in politics, literature, and history, and he wrote many books as well as articles for magazines and newspapers.

He ran for president in 1972, 1976, 1988, and 1992, and, though none of these races had the impact of 1968, he was still able to affect some change.

Abigail and Gene were separated in 1969. While they lived apart, they never divorced. Abigail became an author and columnist who championed women's causes. She died February 1, 2001, in Washington, D.C.

McCarthy continues to urge for changing the eight-hour workday to six hours. He believes that U.S. foreign policy is inconsistent and that federal fund-raising-limit laws "blatantly violate the freedom of speech."

McCarthy lives on a farm near Washington, D.C., in rural Virginia and maintains an office in Washington. He occasionally returns to Minnesota to visit his brother Austin, a doctor in Willmar.

During an interview for this book, Sen. McCarthy somewhat bemusedly noted that since he left the Senate, only one Minnesota governor has invited him to the Governor's Mansion in St. Paul: Jesse Ventura.

A maverick not afraid to take unpopular positions, Eugene McCarthy works for what he believes is right. He has even taken on the advocacy group Common Cause and John Gardner in opposing limits for campaign spending.

He remains a man of conviction, staunchly believing he was entitled to name his last book, *I'm Sorry I Was Right*. While he says he cannot be proud that he was right about Vietnam, he says that being part of Civil Rights legislation brought a great deal of satisfaction. He says there isn't much point in second guessing political life.

His only advice to school children is to "continue as you're doing. I think kids are doing pretty well today."

Source: Biographical material provided by subject; personal interview by author; *Limits of Power* by Eugene McCarthy, Holt, Rinehart and Winston, New York, 1967.

Kevin McHale
Pro-Basketball Hall of Famer

When Kevin McHale was in seventh grade in Hibbing, Minnesota, he had no thoughts of being a professional basketball player. He was a skinny five-foot-eight-inch kid with a five-foot-ten-inch father and a five-foot-six-inch mother. He just wanted to be a good person. His favorite sport was hockey.

But a surge in growth to six feet, ten inches by his senior year at Hibbing High School changed everything. He would become one of the National Basketball Association's all-time greats.

Born in Hibbing on December 12, 1957, McHale led his high-school team to the Minnesota Class AA Basketball Championship in 1976. Then he fulfilled a dream by accepting a scholarship to the University of Minnesota. He averaged 15.2 points and 8.5 rebounds in his four years with the Gophers. In Kevin's senior year, his team won the National Intercollegiate Tournament Championship.

The legendary Red Auerbach, then president of the Boston Celtics, wanted Kevin on his team. It took some trades and dealings to achieve, but Red was successful. Not only did he land McHale with the third pick overall in the draft, but he also obtained Robert Parrish. With Larry Bird, who was in his second season with the Celtics, the three would form the basis of the most dominating front court in the National Basketball Association (NBA).

Kevin was delighted with his selection by the Celtics. "What better place to play for an Irish-Catholic kid than Boston," he enthused.

For thirteen seasons, Kevin McHale starred for the Boston Celtics, his only professional team. Initially, McHale was used as a sixth man, first off the bench. He played a majority of the game, coming in as a reserve. His first year, he was named to the NBA All-Rookie Team. The Celtics won the 1981 NBA Championship with Kevin playing an important role.

McHale's playing time and points-scored increased, but the Celtics didn't make it back to the NBA finals. For the 1983-1984 season, K.C. Jones became the head coach, and Kevin's play took off. He played 31.4 minutes coming off the bench, averaged 18.4 points and 7.4 rebounds a game. He won the NBA Sixth Man Award and, for the first time, was named to the NBA All-Star Team, an honor he was to repeat six more times. Most importantly, the Celtics beat the Lakers for the NBA Championship.

Throughout the 1980s, the Celtics dominated the Atlantic Division of the NBA and won three national championships. McHale's contributions to their success were vital. He won three Sixth Man Awards, was All-NBA First-Team in 1987, and was named to the NBA All-Defensive First Team three times and the second team three other times.

Once McHale scored fifty-six points in a game. Twice he blocked nine shots in a game. For his career, Kevin averaged 17.9 points per game and shot 54.4 per cent from the field and 79.8 percent from the free throw line.

In his best year, 1987, McHale averaged 26.1 points and 9.9 rebounds in addition to capturing the best field goal percentage title, the first of two such achievements.

His skill brought fame and recognition beyond the basketball court. The television program *Cheers* featured him in cameo roles in two episodes. In one memorable segment, Kevin's skills declined when, prompted by the *Cheers* gang, he became obsessed with counting the parquet squares on the Boston Garden floor.

In real life, Kevin had a unique encounter at another prominent venue, Madison Square Garden. At the conclusion of a game, McHale looked into the stands and spotted Bob Dylan, also one of Hibbing's famous sons. The legendary singer, a man of few words, looked down at McHale, nodded his head, and said only one word: "Hibbing."

Often the most meaningful tributes to McHale have come from opponents. Charles Barkley, another NBA great, described Kevin as, "The toughest guy I have ever played against." Hubie Brown, a former NBA coach, told the *Boston Globe*, "He became the most difficult low-post player to defend—once he had the ball—in the history of the league."

His fakes and moves from the low-post gave defenders fits. Kevin's exceptionally long arms enabled him to shoot over players who were taller or better jumpers.

Over his last five seasons, Kevin's numbers declined. Foot and ankle injuries led to missed games, fewer minutes, and decreased mobility. Yet, in his last season of 1992-1993, he still averaged 10.7 points a game and nineteen in the first round of the play-offs.

But when Charlotte won game four of the series, eliminating the Celtics, McHale announced his playing days were over. He had scored 17,355 points, grabbed 7,122 rebounds, blocked 1,690 shots, and shot .554 from the field. He was the Celtics' fourth-leading scorer of all time.

Kevin returned to Minnesota and, with his family, moved into a home in North Oaks. In his first year out of pro ball, he worked as a special assistant for the Minnesota Timberwolves and as a television analyst for their games.

Later he was moved up to assistant general manager and, in May of 1995, McHale became vice-president of basketball operations for the Timberwolves.

In his role as an executive, Kevin has been instrumental in building a franchise that finally made the playoffs after many dismal seasons. Through shrewd drafting and trades, his Timberwolves became one of the better teams in the NBA.

In 1999 McHale was elected to the NBA Hall of Fame. On February 18, 1995, the University of Minnesota named him the best player in the first one hundred years of men's basketball at the "U." At the NBA All-Star game in 1997, Kevin was introduced as being one of the NBA's Top Fifty Players for the second half of the century.

In 2000 the Timberwolves broke NBA rules in the signing of a player, Joe Smith. Controversy over Kevin's role in the signing led to his suspension from the team until August 2001.

Kevin and his wife, Lynn, live in North Oaks with their five children, Kristyn, Michael, Joseph, Alexandra, and Thomas.

Kevin relishes the time he had on the court. He played against people he really admired, such as Larry Bird, Magic Johnson, and Bill Walton. He fought to defeat the "tough" teams, like Philadelphia, L.A., and Detroit. He says that playing basketball is the most enjoyable thing he has ever done, and management is not the same. He marvels at how hard it is to keep a team together today, especially with the outside interests of the players. He still tries to spend time with his family.

His advice to school children is, "Get a great education—try to be the best possible person you can be."

Source: Biographical material provided by Minnesota Timberwolves, Timberwolves Website, *The Case for Kevin McHale,* by Kent Wipf; NBA Website.

Vern Mikkelsen
Pro-Basketball Hall of Famer

By today's standards, Vern Mikkelsen did it all wrong. He came from a tiny town, didn't specialize in one sport, didn't lift weights, didn't go to a major university, and didn't even see a real basketball court or game until he was in the seventh grade.

But Mikkelsen became a phenomenally successful basketball player, an All-American in college, a professional all-star who defined a whole new position, and an NBA Hall of Famer.

It all began in the tiny northern Minnesota town of Askov. Located near Duluth, the town of 300 people (mostly Danish) needed a new minister for the Danish Lutheran church. A call went out to Pastor Michael Mikkelsen. With his wife, two daughters, and son Vern, the pastor began his service to the Askov congregation.

Vern, a seventh grader, involved himself in the school and community. The small school needed most of its students to be active if it was to have extracurricular activities. Vern heard the frequent entreaty, "We need you." Thus, he participated in a variety of activities, including four years in the school play.

Academically, he was proud to be fourth in his graduating class, until he realized that didn't even place him in the top third.

Leading up to his final year in high school, Mikkelsen was average in size and enjoyed playing basketball. As a senior, he gained more presence on the court, sprouting to six-feet five-inches and 180 pounds. He became a dominant high-school player and attracted the attention of college coaches.

The youth from Askov seemed poised to attend the University of Minnesota upon high-school graduation in 1945. But six foot, nine inch Jim McIntyre enrolled at the "U." Vern decided better opportunities might lie elsewhere.

Coaches at Hamline University in St. Paul had assured him a starting position at center. During a time when church affiliation was emphasized even at the college level, the Danish Lutheran Mikkelsen enrolled to become a Piper at the Methodist university.

"My parents supported me totally," Vern related. "They were immigrants from Denmark. My father being a Danish Lutheran minister, my enrolling in a school like Hamline was kind of a opposite direction.

"A Lutheran going to a Methodist school could have caused some problems, but it didn't, because my parents were so supportive."

A sixteen-year-old freshman, Mikkelsen was coached at Hamline by Joe Hutton.

"He was an outstanding coach. We played a national schedule then. It was before Divisions 1, 2, or 3."

"We played East Coast, West Coast, Chicago Stadium, Boston, Madison Square Garden. I started as a freshman and went on from there. Joe Hutton was a big influence on me."

Mikkelsen had a great basketball career at Hamline, averaging 16.7 points as a junior and 17.3 as a senior. Hamline won the NAIA Championship Vern's senior year, and he was twice named an All-American. With all that, he still found time to join the a cappella choir.

Mikkelsen graduated from Hamline in 1949. That same year, the Basketball Association of America and the National Basketball League were competing for players. The Anderson Packers of the NBL wanted Vern, but so did the BBA's Minneapolis Lakers, who made Mikkelsen a territorial draft pick.

Vern chose to play with the Lakers. He signed for $6,000 and a $1,500 bonus. He went out and paid cash for a brand new Pontiac. The next fall, the BBA absorbed the NBL to become the National Basketball Association. With stars Jim Pollard and George Mikan, the Lakers had been BBA champions in 1948-1949. The addition of the twenty-year-old Mikkelsen, now six-foot seven-inches and 230 pounds, made the Lakers virtually unbeatable. It also formed the basis of one of sports' first great dynasties.

With two other rookies, Slater Martin and Bobby Harrison, joining Minneapolis at the same time as Mikkelsen, the Lakers won four national championships in the next five years.

"I ended up teaming up with Mikan and Pollard, and the rest is history," Vern explained. "Mikan dominated the game. He was the Michael Jordan, Magic Johnson, and Larry Bird all rolled into one in our era. George was the foundation of the NBA.

"He was a great teammate and great friend. It was a wonderful experience."

As a rookie, Vern spelled Mikan in the center spot. On occasion, the Lakers experimented with a double pivot, using both Mikan and Mikkelsen at the same time. That didn't work well, so the Lakers found another way to get Vern in the line-up. Their solution was to create the position of power forward for Mikkelsen.

Vern had only played center in college. "We didn't dribble, we didn't shoot from outside, we got under the hoop and rebounded. They wanted me to be a double pivot with George, and that didn't work at all. It just crammed everything together.

"So they moved me out to the side and turned me around to face the basket. I ended up learning how to be a power forward before there was a name for it.

"Most of my scoring came from rebounding. I developed an outside shot after I got with the Lakers. I had a little two-hand set-shot from the outside that kept the defense honest."

The power forward position wasn't the only innovation brought about by the Minneapolis Lakers. To prevent teams from stalling to keep the ball away from the potent Laker offense, the twenty-four-second clock was established. To lessen the impact of the big men like Mikan in the middle, the lane under the basket was widened from six feet to twelve and later to fifteen, where it now remains.

The first half of Mikkelsen's career was especially grinding. The teams traveled by train for their schedule of sixty-eight games. It wasn't uncommon to play a game in Rochester, New York, on a Saturday night, and then travel by train to Minneapolis for a Sunday night game.

"We got used to it," Vern related. "We were like zombies after the first month."

The Lakers won three consecutive championships from 1952 to 1954, and a total of five in six years. Vern was amazingly consistent in his scoring and rebounding. He was among the leaders in each category for most of the years that he played.

Even more impressive was Mikkelsen's durability. He played in 642 consecutive games. From the 1951-1952 season through his retirement following the 1958-1959 season, he played in every one of the team's 715 games, including the post season. With contests before 1951-1952 included, he totaled 699 of 704 regular-season games.

This was before the days of the conditioning regimen of modern athletes. Weightlifting was believed to lead to becoming "musclebound." So Vern devised his own program to stay in shape. He ran, skipped rope, worked out with gymnastics drills, and did one hundred fingertip push-ups a day. It paid off.

Mikkelsen had his best statistical season in 1954-1955, when he scored 18.7 points a game. He earned a master's degree in psychology from the University of Minnesota that same year.

By the 1957-1958 season, things were different for the Lakers. Pollard and Mikan had retired. Slater Martin was traded, Harrison was gone, and Mikkelsen became the leader of a very young team.

While Vern did his share with 17.3 points per game and 11.2 rebounds per game, the team slumped to the worst record in the league, 19-53. One of the talented youngsters joining the Lakers was a future hall of famer, Elgin Baylor. Baylor joined Mikkelsen for one final great run in 1958-1959. His last year was a special one for Vern.

"Before, we were expected to win. There were no surprises. My most interesting year was my last year, 1959. Johnny Kundla, my coach, and I were the only ones left from the old days. With Elgin Baylor, we went on to win the Western Division Championship.

"We played the Boston Celtics in the finals. We didn't win, but the season had more of an impact on me, because we weren't expected to win. It was more fun."

Mikkelsen played his greatest game in his last season. He poured in forty-three points against the Cincinnati Royals on February 10. His salary that season was $12,000.

In his ten years in the NBA, Vern was named an All-Star six times. He averaged 14.4 points per game, scoring a career total of 10,156. Mikkelsen snagged 5,940 rebounds as a pro, an average of 9.4 per game.

After the 1958-1959 campaign, the Minneapolis Lakers moved to Los Angeles. Vern was offered an opportunity to become a player-coach. He decided to retire from basketball and remain in Minnesota.

What does Mikkelsen regard as the biggest change in basketball at its various levels from when he played? "The three-point arc," he responded. "The ball used to go from the outside in, that was the offense. Now it goes inside and then comes out. Now they spend eighteen seconds moving the ball around to get an outside shot."

After he retired from playing, Mikkelsen made a brief return to the professional ranks in 1968 as the general manager of the Minnesota Pipers of the American Basketball Association.

During his younger days, Vern had prepared for the time when he would no longer play professional sports. Planning to go into teaching, he had earned a bachelor's degree in education before achieving his master's degree.

However, while a Laker, he had also bought into a small insurance agency, and that became his profession after basketball. Even though the insurance business was successful for Mikkelsen, he still wonders if teaching might not have been a more satisfying career for him.

Vern married Jean Hanson, a young woman from Spicer, Minnesota, in June of 1955. They have two sons, both of whom live on the West Coast. Vern and Jean live in Minnetonka, Minnesota. Vern has been active in fundraising the last few years. He helped to raise money for a new field house at Hamline University, for the Danish Immigrant Museum in Decorah, Iowa, and for a statue of his old teammate and friend, George Mikan.

In 1995, Mikkelsen became the first native Minnesotan named to the NBA Hall of Fame. Five other Laker teammates have been so honored; they include Mikan, Pollard, Martin, Baylor, and Clyde Lovellette. Vern entered the Hall, fittingly, with his coach, John Kundla. Having to wait so long made induction into the Hall even more meaningful for Vern.

"To have the kids, my friends, family, and Hamline friends come and be part of the hall of fame was really very special," he said.

Mikkelsen, the almost-teacher, has this advice for the students of today:

"Participate, be involved. Be part of everything. Don't just concentrate on basketball because you want to be a pro-basketball player. If it happens, that's fine. But get involved in as many different things as you can. Not just sports, but other activities, including the church."

Source: nba.com; Interview with Vern Mikkelsen.

Walter F. Mondale
Vice-President and United States Ambassador

He was a case study in being in the right place at the right time. Four times in his career, powerful men named him to important positions: first attorney general of Minnesota; next U.S. senator from Minnesota; then candidate for vice-president of the United States, and, finally, ambassador to Japan.

But Walter Frederick "Fritz" Mondale used his considerable abilities to make the most of his opportunities as he helped to lead his state and nation.

Walter was born to Theodore Sigvaard and Claribel Cowen Mondale on January 5, 1928, in Ceylon, a small town located in the southeast corner of Minnesota.

As his father was a minister, Fritz's family moved throughout small towns in southern Minnesota. Fritz graduated from high school in Elmore. In 1946, while a student at Macalester College in St. Paul, he met a young man who was running for mayor of Minneapolis. His name was Hubert H. Humphrey.

Humphrey inspired young Mondale to become involved in politics. He worked in Hubert's victorious campaign and began to organize student Democrats.

Throughout the next few years, Fritz mixed his education with political activity. He worked for Hubert Humphrey in his U.S. Senate campaign in the Second District. Mondale aided Orville Freeman in Freeman's unsuccessful bid for attorney general, then worked for him again when Freeman was elected governor in 1954.

Mondale was a political pro seasoned beyond his years when he graduated from the University of Minnesota in 1951. After earning his degree, Fritz completed service as a corporal in the U.S. army and went to law school at the University of Minnesota. He began to practice law in Minneapolis.

On June 21, 1955, Mondale met Joan Adams on a blind date. On December 27 of that same year, they were married in a ceremony performed by Joan's father, a Presbyterian minister.

The climb up the governing ladder began in 1960, when Governor Orville Freeman appointed Walter Mondale to serve as Minnesota Attorney General after Miles Lord resigned. Fritz was elected to the office two years later.

Fritz gained the opportunity to hold national office four years later. In 1964, President Lyndon Johnson named U.S. Senator Hubert Humphrey to be his vice-presidential candidate on the Democratic ticket, which went on to score an overwhelming victory over the Republican ticket of Arizona Governor Barry Goldwater and U.S. Rep. William Miller of New York.

Humphrey's election to the vice-presidency created a vacant U.S. Senate position. Governor Karl Rolvaag selected Mondale to fill out Humphrey's term. In 1966 and again in 1972, the voters of Minnesota confirmed Rolvaag's decision by returning Mondale to the Senate.

While a senator, Fritz Mondale worked to end segregation through open housing and through busing for school children. He was named chairman of the select committee on Equal Education Opportunity in 1970. Mondale forced an examination of whether public schools were providing equal opportunity for a decent education.

He also chaired a Senate subcommittee on migrant labor. The committee uncovered deplorable conditions and exploitation among the migrant workers. Mondale said, "A migrant camp is a microcosm of every social ill . . . every injustice . . . everything shameful in our society."

On the Senate floor in 1972, Mondale turned the focus of school integration to the educational institutions of the North, saying, "School desegregation in the South is largely completed. But we from the North are now beginning to feel the pressure, which our colleagues from the South felt for so many years, to abandon the course set by the Fourteenth Amendment. If we do, we will deal a blow to public education in the North and South from which it may never recover."

In 1976, Democratic presidential candidate Jimmy Carter selected the man from Elmore to run with him as vice-president. The team was elected. Mondale became the first vice-president to have an office in the White House.

Vice-President Mondale's Senate experience served him in good stead. He served as a full-time participant, advisor, and troubleshooter for Carter, both at home and abroad. Fritz became a spokesman for President Carter on Capitol Hill, supporting legislation to increase minimum wages, reform labor law, and tighten controls of United States intelligence operations.

The highlight of Walter's career as vice-president was the signing of the Camp David Peace Accords between Israel and Egypt. "That was a thrilling day!"

Joan Mondale became one of America's greatest advocates for the arts. She served as honorary chairman of the Federal Council on the Arts and Humanities.

But problems plagued the Carter administration, among them the Iran hostage drama, brought about when U.S. embassy personnel were captured and held hostage in Iran. The Republican duo of Ronald Reagan and George Bush crushed Carter-Mondale in their re-election bid in 1980.

Mondale returned to the practice of law in Washington, D.C. Still, he yearned for a shot at the White House on his own. In 1984, he became the Democratic nominee for president of the United States.

His campaign broke ground. Mondale named U.S. Representative Geraldine Ferraro of New York as his running mate, making her the first woman ever selected to run on a national ticket. Typically aware of his roots, Mondale brought Ferraro to his hometown of Elmore and to the porch of his boyhood home. But Reagan-Bush won the election with a comfortable margin.

Minnesotan Paul Ridgeway, who worked as an advance man on the campaign, described Mondale as "very thoughtful and bright. He cares about people."

For the next several years, Walter Mondale practiced law, taught, studied, and traveled. In 1987 he returned to Minnesota to join the law firm of Dorsey & Whitney.

In 1993 President Clinton nominated Mondale to be U.S. ambassador to Japan. He served there for three years, helping to negotiate trade agreements and the U.S. military presence in Okinawa.

After returning to Dorsey & Whitney in 1996, Mondale continued to serve as a special envoy for President Clinton and to conduct public forums on government.

Fritz and Joan continued to reside in the Twin Cities. They have three children: William, Eleanor, and Ted, who has been a state senator and currently is chairman of the Metropolitan Council.

Walter's advice for school children is, "I tell young people to follow their heart, do what they want to do and to have high aspirations. If you do that, you will get better every day." He was taught as a child that everyone is equal and equally deserving of respect and fair treatment, he felt privileged to spend his life promoting those values.

Source: Biographical data provided by Dorsey and Whitney; interviews with associates.

Dr. John S. Najarian

Transplant Surgeon

The twelve-year-old boy was desperately sick. His appendix had ruptured, poisoning his system. For the next six weeks, he would spend most of his time slowly recovering in a hospital bed.

Out of his pain and suffering, the boy came to admire the doctors and nurses who cared for him. Then and there, he decided that he wanted to do something in the medical profession.

The boy was John S. Najarian. He would become one of America's foremost transplant surgeons and chairman of the Surgery Department at the University of Minnesota Hospital.

Najarian was a 1948 honors graduate of the University of California at Berkeley. He went on to the University of California, San Francisco, where he earned his M.D. in 1952 and completed his general surgical training in 1960.

For one year, Najarian did research in immunopathology at the University of Pittsburgh. He followed that with a year of tissue transplantation immunology at Scripps Clinic and Research Foundation. He became a Markle Scholar of Academic Medicine.

All transplant surgeons have to graduate from four years of college, then four years of medical school, followed by five or six years of surgical training, and, finally, followed by an additional two years of transplant training. This training does include practice on animals.

John served as director of Surgical Research Laboratories and chief of the Transplantation Service (1963 to 1966) and then professor and vice-chairman (1966 to 1967) of the Surgery Department at the University of California, San Francisco.

He moved to the University of Minnesota in 1967. There he became professor and chairman of the Surgery Department. Dr. Najarian made the University of Minnesota Hospital's transplant program one of the world's largest. Through this program, more than 5,000 kidney transplants were performed; more than 1,000 pancreas transplants; and hundreds of heart, liver, lung, islet of Langerhans, bowel, and combined transplants. Dr. Najarian has personally performed over 2,700 transplants.

Under Dr. Najarian's leadership, the Minnesota program pioneered new and difficult types of transplants; achieved unequaled success with diabetic, pediatric and older patients; and made major research, clinical and educational contributions to the field of surgery.

He notes that few people die from transplant surgery. However, he does admit to operating on some famous people, including a liver transplant for Jamie Fiske eighteen years ago when she was only eleven months old (and she's still doing very well), and put a kidney into Gene Okerlund, who is an announcer for the WWF.

Honors have followed him. Internationally, Dr. Najarian was admitted as an Honorary Fellow to the Royal College of Surgeons of England in 1987. Only a few surgeons throughout the world share that distinction. The University of Minnesota awarded him its highest honor in 1985, when it named him a Regent's Professor. In 1986, the university endowed him with the Jay Phillips Distinguished Chair in Surgery. His most recent award is the Roche Pioneer Award, which he received in 1999. It's given by the American Society of Transplant Surgeons in recognition of a lifetime contribution to transplantation.

Minnesota and worldwide agencies have continued to bestow awards and honors upon Dr. Najarian for the work he has done. But throughout all this, he has remained a decent, approachable man.

A tree-nursery owner, Dick Cambronne of nearby Hudson, Wisconsin, recounted a conversation he had with Dr. Najarian when he planted some trees on the doctor's property. The nursery owner asked where he should dig the holes. Dr. Najarian, not presuming to know the landscaping business, replied, "You're the professional here. Me telling you where the best place to put the trees would be like you telling me where to make the incision for an operation."

Dr. Najarian is married to a Minnesota native, whom he met in California while she was working as a nurse. Dr. Najarian and Mignette have four sons: Jon, Paul, David, and Peter. Peter played linebacker for the Minnesota Gophers football team and went on to play pro-football, including a stint with the Minnesota Vikings.

Dr. Najarian was editor-in-chief of *Clinical Transplantation*, associate editor of *American Journal of Surgery*, and an editorial board member of fifteen other medical journals. He has published more than 1,300 articles and several books.

Also at that time, Dr. Najarian was a clinical professor of surgery and Regent's Professor Emeritus at Fairview-University Medical Center, actively devoted to his main passion: patient care.

"My most satisfaction as a doctor comes from being able to help the sick and having the opportunity to see them get well."

Dr. Najarian's advice for school children is, "I think you need to find an occupation that you enjoy and if it's one in which you can help other people, it's even more satisfying. The most important thing is to get good grades so that you will be able to be admitted to a university, and, if a post-graduate education is indicated in your future, then getting good grades in college will help you achieve admission to law school, medical school, architectural school."

Sources: Biographical information provided by subject; interviews with acquaintances.

Lou Nanne
Hockey Player and Businessman

Minnesota is proud to call itself the "State of Hockey." Many legendary names are associated with the development of the sport in the North Star State. Names like John Mariucci, John Mayasich, and Herb Brooks are etched in lore and history for their contributions.

But for today's fans, perhaps no name conjures up thoughts of ice and vulcanized rubber more than that of Lou Nanne.

Nanne is from Sault Sainte Marie, Ontario, Canada, where he was born on June 2, 1941. "My folks were a big influence on my life," Lou remembered. "They helped me learn a work ethic. They laid the foundation for my life. They were also determined that I get a college degree."

But during his youth, hockey was Louie's first love. He was a "huge fan" of Detroit Red Wings star Gordie Howe. Lou spent endless hours skating with friends, who included future National Hockey League stars Tony and Phil Esposito.

Nanne's skills were recognized at an early age. When he was thirteen, the Chicago Blackhawks obtained rights to him as a hockey player. They wanted Nanne to go to Hamilton and play junior hockey. But Lou, "Sweet Lou from the Soo," as he became known, played juvenile hockey in Sault Saint Marie until graduating from high school in 1959.

Then, fulfilling his parent's dream for him, Nanne went to college. He entered the University of Minnesota, where John Mariucci coached him.

"John was like a second father to me," Lou said. "He drove me to become the best that I could be."

For four years, Nanne starred under Mariucci's tutelage. His senior year, Louie was captain of the Gopher squad, became the first defenseman to lead the league in scoring as he racked up seventy-four points, was named an All-American, and was chosen league MVP. To top it off, he also became an American citizen and earned a degree in business.

But he wasn't ready to play pro hockey. After Louie left the University in 1963, Chicago still owned his rights. The ensuing contract dispute between Nanne and the Hawks left Louie on the sidelines of pro hockey.

Lou sat out for five years. He worked for Harvey MacKay's envelope company, coached the Gopher freshman hockey players for four years, and played some hockey for the Rochester (Minnesota) Mustangs of the USHL.

A highlight of those years was the 1968 Olympics. Lou captained the American team in Grenoble, France. At the start of the 1967-68 season, the NHL expanded. A new reserve list cost Chicago their rights to Lou, and he became a free agent. Nanne signed with the North Stars, Minnesota's new entry in the NHL. He joined the team in March of 1968 after the Olympics.

Nanne would be the only player to play in each of the Stars' first eleven seasons. A steady and physical defenseman and an excellent penalty killer, he made an art of blocking opponents' shots. Usually playing defense, occasionally forward, Nanne totaled seventy-two goals and 167 assists for 239 points in his North Star career.

Known as a team player, Lou worked in labor relations as well. He served a stint as vice-president of the NHL Players' Association. Lou was also captain of the 1975 and 1977 USA World National Hockey teams and assistant captain in 1976. He played for the United States in the 1977 Canada Cup Series. Later, Lou was general manager for the U.S. squad in the Canada Cup in 1981, 1984, and 1987. He served in a similar capacity for the 1994 World Championships.

In February of 1978, Nanne was named coach and general manager of the North Stars. He would coach the final couple months of the season and then manage the team full time.

Lou was known for boldness and innovation in his dealings as general manager. In the 1979 expansion draft, he claimed Dave Sememko from the Edmonton Oilers for the sole purpose of trading him back to the Oilers. The deal included one key stipulation: Edmonton had to leave Neal Broten alone in the amateur draft. Nanne also became prominent at the league level. He served a term as chairman of the General Managers Committee and was an alternate on the NHL's Board of Governors.

Lou was also instrumental in negotiations with the World Hockey League that brought four new teams into the NHL. He did all this while making the North Stars better.

Twice under Lou's leadership, the Stars made the finals of hockey's Holy Grail, the Stanley Cup. In 1988, Nanne resigned as general manager to assume the duties of team president. He served the Stars in that capacity until 1991, when he left to join the business world.

Nanne's hockey career had been long and illustrious. From "the Soo," to college, to Olympics, then as a player, coach, GM, and president at the pro level, he did it all.

What did he like the most? "Playing," Lou responded. "Anytime you can get paid to do what you love is great."

What was the most satisfying? That was harder for Lou to answer. He mentioned the Stanley Cup series, college, the pros and the Olympics. In summary, Lou said, "It just kind of all evolved. It's hard to say if anything was more satisfying than something else."

The respect shown Nanne by his peers is evident in the honors bestowed upon him. In 1980 he was awarded the Lester Patrick Award for his outstanding service to hockey in the United States. Lou was named to the Fifty-Year Western Collegiate Hockey Conference All-Star Team. He was inducted into the United States Hockey Hall of Fame in 1998.

Lou has remained in the business world since 1991. He is currently an executive vice-president and national sales manager for Voyageur Asset Management in Minneapolis.

Lou and his wife, Francine, whom he married in 1964, have four grown children, Michelle, Michael, Mark, and Marty, plus eleven grandchildren. While playing and managing hockey are in his past, Louie still is prominent to hockey fans. Each year, at "March Madness" time in Minnesota, Lou lends his voice and insight as a television analyst for the state hockey tournament. He has also done some network hockey broadcasting and worked on "Hockey Night in Canada."

Lou has been a member of the International Committee for USA Hockey. The man who dreamed of success in hockey offers similar advice to kids of today. Louie advised, "Work hard in school, play for fun and allow yourself to dream.

Source: Interview with Lou Nanne; www.northstarhockey.com; *Frozen Memories*, by Ross Bernstein, p. 51, Nordin Press, Minneapolis, 1999.

George (Pinky) Nelson
Astronaut and Scientist

Tremendous noise and vibration roared through the cabin of the aircraft as something resembling a gigantic explosion shook it. Instantly, an acceleration three times the force of gravity rocketed the craft into the atmosphere.

The first Minnesotan in space looked down as the blue-green sphere below shrank smaller and smaller. Pinky Nelson was certainly a long way from Willmar, Minnesota.

Pinky was born July 13, 1950, in Charles City, Iowa. He was raised in Willmar, where he graduated from high school in 1968. His name was George, but everyone called him Pinky.

A longtime interest in science led him to Harvey Mudd College in California, where he earned a bachelor of science degree in physics in 1972. Nelson chose the University of Washington for his continued education, a master of science and a doctor of astronomy in 1974 and 1978, respectively.

The same year that Nelson earned his doctorate, the National Aeronautics and Space Administration chose him as an astronaut candidate. He was twenty-eight years old.

Pinky flew as a scientific equipment operator in the WB 57-F Earth Resources aircraft and served as the photographer in the prime chase plane for the first space shuttle mission, STS-1.

He worked at various tasks for NASA, but the opportunity for which Nelson longed didn't arrive until April 6, 1984, when he blasted into space aboard the *Challenger*.

During their seven-day flight, Pinky and the crew successfully walked in space, retrieved a malfunctioning satellite, repaired it on board the *Orbiter*, and replaced it in orbit. They also deployed a TV relay satellite.

Pinky Nelson was on two more shuttle flights. A six-day mission aboard *Columbia* in 1986 included a night landing. 1988 brought four days on *Discovery*, the first mission after the disastrous accident that killed seven astronauts aboard the *Challenger*. Dr. Nelson's duties included conducting astrophysics and materials processing experiments, as well as following the flight plan and walking in space.

Pinky does admit that he became sick on his last flight, although he adds that all astronauts do not feel one hundred percent for at least the first two hours.

Life in space is very different. For example, sleep is executed without lying down, and the sun comes up every ninety minutes. Most of what the astronauts consume is freeze-dried. They eat irradiated meat and some fresh fruits and veggies. Also space toilets run on airflow, not gravity like on earth.

Each launch can provide moments of apprehension for an astronaut. Pinky has indicated that his owns "fears" were greatest during takeoff. Yet even after the fatal launch of *Challenger*, as an astronaut, Pinky knew that he had to accept the risks. Danger is simply part of the job. Astronauts are trained to deal with failures, so that, even though something failed on each of Pinky's missions, they were able to work around the problem.

When Nelson retired from the space program in 1989, he had flown 411 hours in space and walked in space twice.

Prior to joining NASA, Pinky married Susan Lynn Howard of Alhambra, California. Their two children are Aimee Tess and Marti Ann. After leaving NASA, Dr. Nelson took the position of director of the American Association for the Advancement of Science's "Project 2061." He remained at that post, developing long-term strategies in research and development and building alliances between scientific and education communities.

Dr. Nelson served as associate professor of astronomy and of education at the University of Washington in Seattle, where he was also assistant provost for research.

Dr. Nelson maintains strong interest in national science education reform. In speeches he has stressed the importance of applied science and the key role that universities have in transferring research into practical applications to meet the needs of our nation and the states.

Pinky's office is in Washington, D.C. His leisure activities include playing golf, reading, cycling, and music. In the summer of 2000, he marked his fiftieth birthday with an earthbound adventure. He and a friend biked from Washington, D.C., to Washington State.

Pinky's hometown of Willmar paid tribute to its astronaut alumnus. On February 25, 2000, a ceremony was held in his honor at Willmar Senior High School. The event featured the public unveiling of a statue by noted wood sculptor Fred Cogelow.

The artist chose to depict Nelson in his NASA uniform. Astride a horse, riding double with a mythical muse, the sculpted Pinky waves a cowboy hat as he gallops toward the stars.

Pinky's advice for school children is, "Be passionate about your interests. Don't be afraid to fail. Personal relationships are very important. Real joy and satisfaction come from working as hard as you can on what is most important to you. Learn how to learn, always demand evidence and think for yourself."

George "Pinky" Nelson

Sources: George (Pinky) Nelson Website; interviews with family members and friends.

Earl B. Olson

Businessman

Earl Olson had time to think about his future. He was hospitalized for eight months after the creamery he managed caught fire. He suffered third-degree burns in the blaze.

As he managed the facility from his hospital bed, Earl determined that there must be ways to increase his income; after all, he was making only one hundred dollars a month and one percent of gross sales. An agricultural empire grew out of the misfortune of the fire when Earl Olson decided to augment his income by raising turkeys.

Olson was born May 8, 1915, in Minnesota's Swift County. He was the son of a Swedish immigrant, Olav, and an American, Anna Carlson. Earl grew up on the Olson farm and went to school in Murdock until the eighth grade.

Earl continued his education at the West Central School of Agriculture in Morris, Minnesota, where he graduated in 1932. Six years later, he married Dorothy Erickson in Murdock.

During the 1940s, he worked for the creamery. After the fire, he bought 1,000 turkeys as a side income. He sold them, earning a profit of one dollar per bird. The next year he bought 3,000 turkeys; the next, he increased it to 5,000. Both batches sold for a profit of one dollar per turkey. They were black turkeys, and the market was very seasonal, depending greatly on sales at Thanksgiving and Christmas.

Olson's business kept growing. The fourth year in it, he made a profit of four dollars per bird on 12,000 turkeys. Then the business took a skid, and Earl lost $60,000 in the fifth year of his enterprise.

But Earl kept persevering, and success followed. He bought a turkey-processing facility in Willmar and renamed it the Farmers Produce Company Olson intentionally wanted it to sound like a cooperative.

In the beginning the "Produce" bought and sold turkeys, chickens, butter, and eggs. Before long, Olson was dealing only in turkeys.

Earl said, "The timing was good; the turkey industry was in its infancy." The Midwest's supply of good, cheap grain aided the growth of the poultry industry.

From its beginnings, Olson's company was innovative in its products. In the early 1950s, the first further-processed product was created: a nine-pound log of turkey called Tur-King that was purchased by the U.S. military.

A great marketing ploy was announced in 1953, when Olson began selling his turkeys as "Jennie-O" in honor of his only daughter, Jennifer. Jennie-O became the official company name in 1971.

The company continued to grow and prosper. However, the cost of expansion became troublesome. In 1986, Earl sold his business to Hormel.

But Jennie-O, although part of Hormel Foods, continued to maintain a separate identity within the parent company.

Earl B. Olson maintains a position as chairman of Jennie-O. In his eighties, Earl still drives to work several times a week. His plain office gives no clue that he built a 500-million-dollar business based on his simple strategy: "New markets and new products."

Jennie-O employs 1,500 in Willmar alone. It has several processing plants in other Minnesota cities and produces millions of birds on Central Minnesota farms.

The results are staggering. Jennie-O processes more than 850 million pounds annually. It is the largest turkey processor in the United States and maybe even the world, much of it because one man dared to dream from his hospital bed.

Success hasn't changed Earl Olson very much. He's a kind man who cares deeply about his country and his community. He gives generously to political causes, community projects, educational institutions, and churches. Every Christmas, he sends checks to fifteen area churches. In April 2000, Earl contributed one and one-half million dollars toward the construction of a YMCA in Willmar.

Dorothy died on July 17, 2000, after an extended illness. She had dedicated her lifetime to family, community, and church.

Earl and Dorothy had five children: Jeffery, Charles, Bruce, Jennifer, and Michael. Earl spends some time in the South each winter but continues to live in Willmar and in a home on Green Lake near Spicer.

Earl's advice to school children is, "Stay in school, continue your education and work hard."

Sources: Seventh grade student Maggie Campe helped write this segment. *Minneapolis Star Tribune*, "Something to Gobble About at Jennie-O," by Ann Merrill, July 16, 1999; Maggie Campe interview with Earl B. Olson.

Lute Olson
National Championship College Basketball Coach

Coach Lute Olson is one of the most respected and successful college basketball coaches in America today. He has won over 600 games at the helm of Division I teams. Olson launched his coaching career in Minnesota.

Born in 1934 on a farm outside Mayville, North Dakota, Lute decided while he was a sophomore in high school that he wanted to be a basketball coach someday.

Lute had an early taste of the thrill of success in that sport. After attending school in Mayville through his junior year, Lute moved with his family to nearby Grand Forks. There he led his team to the 1952 state basketball championship.

College took him to Minneapolis, where young Olson attended Augsburg College. He excelled in three sports at the private Lutheran school, lettering in football, basketball, and baseball. While there, he met his future wife, Roberta Russell, nicknamed Bobbi.

After graduating from Augsburg in 1956, Lute set out towards his goal by coaching at two Minnesota high schools, Mahnomen and Two Harbors. He spent five years honing his skills with Minnesota prepsters. Then Olson and his young family moved west.

Lute modeled his coaching after the styles of Coach Wooden of University of California, Los Angeles, Coach Newell of California, and Dean Smith of University of North Carolina.

Lute and Bobbi raised their family of five children in California. For their first seven years there, Lute coached high-school basketball in the Golden State. Then his drive to coach at the college level was rewarded. He was named Long Beach City College head coach.

In four years, there he was named Conference Coach of the Year three times. In 1971 Lute's team won the state junior college championship. This was followed by a 24-2 season at Long Beach State in 1973 to 1974.

Then the University of Iowa tapped Lute to return to the Midwest and help their program rise to Big-Ten greatness. In nine years at Iowa, he led the Hawkeyes to one conference championship and three second-place finishes. Five times his team played in the "Big Dance," the NCAA tournament. In 1980, a Lute Olson-coached team made the Final Four for the first time.

His teams at Iowa went 167-91, but he had raised his children in the West, and when the call came from the University of Arizona, the yearning to go back there was strong. In 1983 Lute left the Big Ten for the Pac 10 and the Wildcats of Arizona in Tucson. He departed as the winningest coach in University of Iowa history.

His first year, he maybe had doubts about his decision. The Wildcats finished fifth with a record of 11-17. But Coach Olson quickly righted the ship. The next year, the University of Arizona finished in a tie for third in the Pac 10 and began a string of seventeen straight NCAA Tournament appearances for teams coached by Lute Olson. In total, he has brought twenty-two teams to the "Bid Dance."

Three times the Wildcats reached the Final Four, culminating with a NCAA championship with a win over Kentucky in 1997. The victory was truly remarkable. Lute Olson's 1996-97 squad had finished fifth in the Pac 10, the lowest finish since his first year at Arizona. They went into the tournament as a number-four seed with a two-game losing streak. They beat three number-one seeds on the way to the national title. That win is Lute's favorite memory.

In his career at the University of Arizona, Olson's teams won one NCAA championship, played in the Final Four three times and won nine Pac 10 titles; and Lute had been named Conference Coach of the Year six times. Under his tenure, the Wildcats have won twenty games in fourteen consecutive seasons.

His coaching tenure has been amazing. Lute had coached over 800 games and won over 600 of them at the end of the 1999-2001 season. Only thirty-three coaches in NCAA basketball history had won more than 600 games at that time. Coach Olson held just about every coach mark there is to hold in University of Arizona basketball, achieving over 400 victories at the University of Arizona at that season's end.

Coaching honors have been heaped upon the Arizona coach, including the Chase Winged Foot Award, an honor presented to the coach of the national championship team by the New York Athletic Club. In 1988 and 1990, Lute was named the National Coach of the Year.

But Lute Olson's real pride is the players he coaches. In his eyes, they are more than just players. They are individuals with whom he enjoys working and helping to grow, as people as well as athletes. Lute feels that it is not possible today for most programs to think about paying players more to play, as most are operating in the red.

Olson takes the time to care about the young men who play for him, to donate generously to his alma mater Augsburg and even to answer a questionnaire for a bunch of seventh graders he had never heard of before. But not all of it is fun and games, the demands on one's time, doing the recruiting, public relations, fundraising and dealing with the media are just some of the hardest things that big-time college basketball coaches need to do.

Lute's wife, Bobbi, died in Tuscon of ovarian cancer on January 1, 2001. They had been married forty-seven years.

Lute's advice for school children is, "Work hard at school work and at being a good responsible person."

Source: Media Relations: University of Arizona.

Alan C. Page
Minnesota Supreme Court Justice and
Pro-Football Hall of Famer

Alan Page returned home for a momentous visit in 1988. He was in Canton, Ohio, home of the National Football League Hall of Fame. Alan Page spent his formative years in Canton. Fittingly, on that day in 1988, both the town and the Hall claimed Alan as one of its own.

The occasion was the induction of Alan C. Page as one of football's immortals. Customarily, a former coach or player steps to the podium to speak about an inductee. It said much about Page that the person he chose to speak for him was a principal from a Minneapolis school.

The former Minnesota Vikings great didn't dwell upon football when it was his turn to speak at the ceremony. Instead, he used the occasion to talk about the importance of education in his life.

Page was born August 7, 1945. He attended Central Catholic High School in Canton. His prowess in football led to a scholarship at the University of Notre Dame in South Bend, Indiana. After a stellar career playing for the Irish, he graduated with a degree in political science in 1967.

The Minnesota Vikings of the National Football League made a trade before the 1967 draft. They sent running back Tommy Mason and receiver Hal Bledsoe to the Los Angeles Rams for end Marlin McKeever and their number-one pick in the coming draft. With that pick, the Vikings took Page.

Alan Page joined a Vikings team that was in disarray in 1967. Star quarterback Fran Tarkenton had demanded to be traded, saying that he would again never play for Head Coach Norm Van Brocklin. In short order, both the quarterback and the coach were gone.

Stability returned to the Vikings that year in the presence of a competent new coach, Bud Grant, and in the young, large, but agile defensive lineman, Alan Page.

Alan had a spectacular career with the Vikings. He played with great power but almost always under complete control. This was an amazing combination in the controlled mayhem that is professional football.

With Carl Eller, Gary Larsen, and Jim Marshall, Page was one part of the most awesome "front fours" in NFL history, the Purple People Eaters. The fourth quarter of 1969's conference title game against Los Angeles was a testament to its greatness. In one series, after being wrongfully (in his mind) penalized, Page demolished the Rams' offensive line, sacking their quarterback Roman Gabriel. The Vikings went on to play in their first Super Bowl that year.

In 1971, Page became the first defensive player in NFL history to receive the "Most Valuable Player" award. Numerous awards and honors followed in recognition of his superlative NFL play.

Bud Grant reflected about his All-Pro lineman. "Alan was a great player. He changed the position of defensive tackle. He played end in college, and we moved him inside where he could take advantage of his extreme quickness and be involved in nearly every play. Page redefined the position. Other teams later tried to utilize players the way that we did Page."

But to Alan Page, football was a means to an end. While he was playing football full time, he was also a full-time law student at the University of Minnesota. In 1978, he earned his law degree and became an associate with Lindquist and Vennum in 1979.

Page ended his pro-football career with the Chicago Bears in 1981. Then he returned to Minneapolis to practice law. He dabbled in broadcasting as a commentator for National Public Radio and with Turner Broadcasting System, doing color for the College Football Game of the Week.

In 1985 he became a Special Assistant Attorney General for the State of Minnesota in the Employment Law Division. Two years later, Page was appointed Assistant Attorney General, a position he held until 1993, when he was elected an Associate Justice to the Minnesota Supreme Court.

The Minnesota Supreme Court is made up of seven justices. "We do a lot of reading in preparing to hear a case. We then listen to both parties argue the case, and then meet in a conference to talk about the case and make a decision. Once a decision is reached, an opinion is written by one of the justices."

Page takes his job very seriously. He realizes that what he and his fellow justices decide affects not only the lives of the participants who are bringing their case before the court but life and property for the rest of Minnesota as well.

Alan Page believes in giving back to the community and to programs that aid education, particularly for disadvantaged children of color. To that end, he has devoted time to numerous community activities and professional organizations.

From 1989 to 1992, he served on the University of Minnesota Board of Regents. In 1988, he founded the Page Education Foundation to assist minority and other disadvantaged youth with post-secondary education.

Justice Page is married to Diane Sims Page. They have four children: Nina, Georgi, Justin, and Kamie.

Through much of his career, Alan Page has marched to a different drummer than many of his fellow athletes, for whom football was all consuming. He was a great football player who used the sport to help himself achieve larger, more important goals. Justice Alan Page's commitment to education and to law continues to guide his life as he dons the black robe and interprets the law for over four million Minnesotans.

Alan Page hopes that he will fulfill all of his dreams. He would like the opportunity to be a teacher. "I believe that it would be exciting, challenging and interesting to teach at the law school level. I also think, however, that it would be just as exciting, challenging and interesting to teach at the fourth-grade level."

His advice for school children is that "education is an important key to success. I would encourage every child to concentrate on preparing him or herself for the future so that he or she will be in a position to pursue their dreams. The work done in school today will have a direct bearing on future success. Simply put, with an education, the future is yours."

Source: Minnesota-Supreme-Court-provided biography, interviews.

Gary Paulsen
Author

It's been said that the best stories come from real-life experiences. Gary Paulsen has lived much of what he puts into his books. The reality that jumps from the pages captures the minds of fascinated young readers.

But were it not for one person who cared about a small boy on a cold winter night in a small northern Minnesota town, we might not have heard of Gary Paulsen at all.

Paulsen was born in Minneapolis, Minnesota, on May 17, 1939. Events of World War II soon changed his family life, taking his father overseas to Europe and sending his mother to work in a factory. His father's military career later led to frequent moves for the Paulsen family. Gary spent several of his mid-childhood years living overseas in the Philippines from 1946 to 1949.

Eventually the Paulsens settled in northern Minnesota. But life wasn't happy for Gary. His parents were alcoholics. His home life was terrible. Still young, he moved away from his parents to live with his grandmother and aunts. Although they were supportive, Gary didn't find real comfort until one cold night.

In Gary's words, "I had a miserable home life, and I would sell newspapers to the drunks at the local bars to make a little money. I went into a library one night to get warm, and the librarian asked me if I wanted something. I said no, I just wanted to warm up a little.

"At that point, very few people had ever given me anything. Both my folks were drinking, and it was a rough run. And then the librarian said, 'Do you want a library card?' So I said yeah. She handed me a card with my name on it—my name—which was amazing to me. And then she asked if I wanted a book. I said, 'Sure,' kind of cocky. And she said to bring it back when I was done, and she'd give me another one."

That night changed Gary Paulsen's life. He found his comfort in books. Soon he was reading two a week, from westerns to science fiction and sometimes even a classic.

Life was still hard. Gary had to work to support himself. At fourteen, he traveled with a carnival. He spent sweaty summers working on a farm. Then he attended Bemidji State College, trapping fur-bearing animals to pay for his tuition.

After college, he spent time in the army. He worked at a variety of jobs until landing a position as a satellite technician for an aerospace firm in California. However, the hunger to read, and then to create books, wouldn't leave him. One day in the mid-1960s, Paulsen simply quit his job to become a magazine proofreader. He honed his own writing at night.

After one year of proofreading, he left California, drove to northern Minnesota, rented a cabin by a lake and began to write a book. His first effort, *Special War*, was published in 1966.

His past jobs and future interests provided a rich background from which Gary drew for his stories. He had been, or was to be, a farm worker, rancher, truck driver, sailor, dog sled racer, teacher, field engineer, editor, actor, director, trapper, professional archer, migrant farm worker, and singer.

Most of his books are set in the Northwoods that he knew growing up and are written for young adults. Paulsen wrote of dog sledding from his personal experience in the famed Iditarod Race, the grueling 1,180-mile trek across Alaska.

In 1983 and 1985, he toiled across the snow-packed tundras with his dogs. An angina attack in 1985 and a heart attack in 1990 ended his dog-racing days.

Gary Paulsen lives to write. He works at his books with great dedication, sometimes writing sixteen to eighteen hours a day. The result has been a lot of books, nearly 200, and some 200 magazine articles and short stories. His wife, Ruth Wright Paulsen, an artist, illustrates many of his books.

Gary is driven to write by his belief in young people. He wants them to observe and care about the world around them. Three of his novels—*Hatchet*, *Dogsong*, and *The Winter Room*—were named Newberry Honor books. He is recognized as one of the best authors of young adult literature in America today.

The Paulsens divide their time between a ranch in southern New Mexico and a sailboat in the Pacific. He continues writing and reading. The librarian on that cold, snowy night in Minnesota couldn't have known what showing kindness to a shivering young boy would unleash.

Source: Random House; Gary Paulsen web homepage.

Carl Pohlad
Owner of the Minnesota Twins and Banker

Carl Pohlad was born third of eight children on August 23, 1915, in West Des Moines, Iowa. Carl attended West Des Moines High School.

A lack of straight A's in school was not an accurate measure of young Pohlad's future success. An average student, Carl was an ambitious youth who became involved in business even before graduating from high school. After completing secondary school in Des Moines, Pohlad attended Gonzaga University in Washington State.

His blossoming career as an entrepreneur was interrupted by World War II. Pohlad went to Europe as part of the U.S. army infantry. He fought in combat in France, Germany, and Austria.

At the war's conclusion, Carl returned to Iowa for a short time before moving to Minneapolis in the 1940s. There he became involved in the banking business and, over a fifty-plus-year career, successfully created and expanded a number of important banking interests. Through hard work and shrewd dealings, Carl Pohlad became immensely successful.

Pohlad and his family have numerous investments. They include bank-related service organizations, Marquette Banks, Pepsi Cola franchises, airline passenger and freight operations and—the acquisition that has brought Pohlad his greatest notoriety—the Minnesota Twins of the American Baseball League.

Carl assumed control of the Twins on September 7, 1984, after purchasing them from Calvin Griffith. The Twins were in danger of being sold and moved out of Minnesota. Pohlad bought them, in part because of a deep sense of community responsibility and pride. He believed that it was important to keep professional baseball in Minnesota and build a winning team. In 1987 and 1991, the Twins delivered World Series Championships to their millions of fans.

Pohlad served on two of the most important ownership committees: the Major League Baseball executive council and the Player Relations Committee board of directors. He was elected vice-president of the American League.

For many decades, the business and civic communities of Minneapolis and St. Paul have looked to Carl Pohlad for leadership. He serves as president and director of Marquette Bancshares, as chairman of the board of Mesaba Holdings, Inc., and as director of Champion Air and Genmar Holdings, Inc.

His personal commitment to the Twin Cities and its people was evident when he helped a struggling young immigrant woman start a business in Bloomington. Her name: Leeann Chin.

Beyond his business interests, Pohlad has consistently believed in community involvement, particularly in activities that aid young people. He is a founding member of the board of directors of the Boy's and Girl's Clubs of Minneapolis. Pohlad is also a member of the advisory council at Johns Hopkins Department of Orthopedic Surgery. He is a trustee of the Hugh O'Brian Youth Foundation and, since 1989, has been a member of the Horatio Alger Association of Distinguished Americans, which provides scholarships for graduating high-school seniors.

Pohlad's concern for his community is also evident through his role as a board member of the Methodist Hospital Health System and the Saddat Peace Foundation.

The Twins continue to be the Pohlad family's main passion. Carl's three sons all serve on the nine-member Twins' executive board. "Most people know that I've always had a close relationship with Kirby Puckett and Kent Hrbek. Their families and mine are still close."

Carl has made many friends in baseball, and has many good memories. "If I can pick only one memory, it would be when the Twins returned to Minnesota after winning the American League Championship in October 1987. We were told that a few people were waiting to greet us at the Metrodome. It was very late at night, past midnight, in fact. We arrived at a dark Metrodome. Suddenly, the lights came on and there were more than 50,000 people there to greet us. It was amazing and incredibly heartwarming to know that so many people shared in the joy of our victory."

He and his wife, Eloise, a passionate fan of her husband's team, reside in Edina.

Carl believes the changes in baseball, such as profit sharing and salary caps, will bring about more competitiveness.

Carl's advice to school children is, "Be and accept who you are. Learn what you are good at and develop those skills as much as you can."

Source: Biographical material provided by Minnesota Twins, *2000 Twins Media Guide.*

-

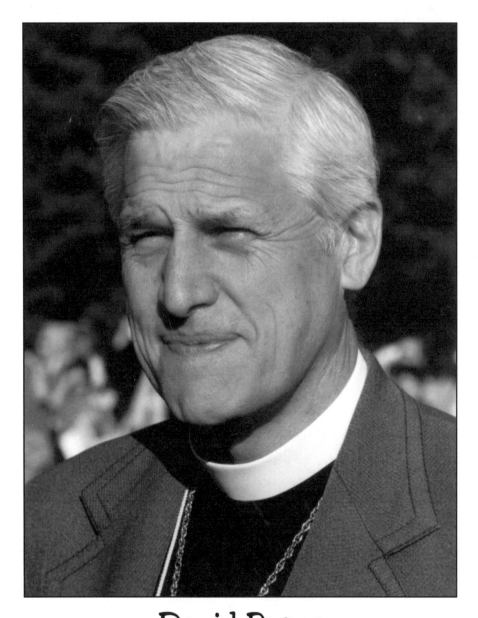

David Preus

Pastor and Bishop of the American Lutheran Church

David Preus was born in Madison, Wisconsin, in 1922. He attended Luther College in Decorah, Iowa, and graduated in 1943, just in time to get in on the latter stages of World War II.

He served his nation in the United States army from 1943 to 1946, with assignments in the Philippine Islands and Japan. Upon his discharge, Preus attended the University of Minnesota Law School for a year. However, after concluding that, he decided to become a pastor and enrolled at Luther Theological Seminary in St. Paul.

He finished his studies at Luther in 1950 and then did graduate studies in theology at the University of Edinburgh, Scotland. For the next twenty-three years, Pastor Preus served congregations in Brookings and Vermillion, South Dakota, and in Minneapolis.

Preus and Ann Madsen were married in 1951 while in Brookings. They had five children: daughters Martha, Louise, and Laura, and sons David A. and Stephen. The family also included seven grandchildren.

Pastor Preus' strong belief in serving his community led to his active participation on many boards and organizations, both church and civic. From 1965 to 1973, he was a member of the Minneapolis School Board, serving two years as president. His years on the school board spanned a turbulent time when Minneapolis struggled with racial desegregation in the 1960s.

Pastor Preus also served on the Minneapolis City Planning Commission, Board of Estimate and Taxation, the Urban Coalition, the Minnesota School Board Association, the Plymouth Christian Youth Center, the Augsburg College Board of Regents, and the executive committee of the Peace Prize Forum.

During his Minneapolis years, he served as pastor of University Lutheran. Then the call to national leadership came from his church.

In 1973 David Preus became presiding bishop of the American Lutheran Church of Hope. He served during a time of great change in the church. During his fifteen years in office, he also served as vice-president of the Lutheran World Federation and on the executive committee of the World Council of Churches.

In 1988, following the merger of the American Lutheran Church into the Evangelical Lutheran Church in America, Bishop Preus was appointed distinguished visiting professor at Luther Seminary in St. Paul and director of its Global Mission Institute.

Bishop Preus has received recognition from many quarters. He was awarded the Commander's Cross, Royal Norwegian Order of St. Olaf; the St. George's Medal of the Orthodox Church of Georgia; the Anti-Defamation League's Torch of Liberty Award; the Minnesota Hall of Fame Award from Temple Israel; the St. Thomas Aquinas Award from the University of St. Thomas; the Pax Christi Award from St. John's University; and ten honorary doctorates from other colleges and universities.

Dr. Preus' family has a tradition of service to God and community. Two brothers also served as pastors.

Preus' advice to school children is, "Love God. Love your neighbor. Find ways to affirm people instead of being critical. Commit yourself to be interested in and doing good for your school, your town, your state, your nation, and the world. Read books. Be a lifelong learner. Discover what a great gift life is and then enjoy it to the hilt."

Preus admires the current prime minister of Norway. "Per capita, Norwegian giving to third world people in need is the highest in the world. Norwegians do more for peace keeping proportionately than any other country. They support United Nations with more dollars per person than any other country . . . perhaps sixteen times as much as the U.S. This has been going on for many years and is an example to all leaders and nations."

Source: Biographical information provided by subject.

Kirby Puckett
Pro-Baseball Hall of Famer

Charlie Leibrandt, Atlanta Braves left-hander, peered from the mound at the short, stocky, muscular hitter standing at the plate. Over 50,000 voices were screaming the batter's name: "KIRBY, KIRBY!"

Leibrandt swung into his windup and fired. Kirby Puckett lifted his front leg slightly and then ripped at the pitch. The ball shot deep to left center, rocketing into the stands.

The next thing millions heard was a television broadcaster shouting, "And we'll see you tomorrow night!" Kirby Puckett, the boy from Chicago, had just ended Game Six of the 1991 World Series with one of the most dramatic home runs in Series history. The Twins and Braves would meet the next night in the deciding Game Seven.

In his twelve-year career, Puckett became the Twins' all-time leader in five categories: hits, doubles, total bases, at-bats, and runs. He was a ten-time American League All-Star. Six times Puckett was awarded a Gold Glove as the league's best defensive center fielder. Five times his hitting was rewarded with a Silver Slugger Award.

Kirby Puckett's story is one about which young athletes dream. Born in the projects of Chicago in 1962, Puckett became what many believe to be the greatest Twin ever.

It almost didn't happen. It's tough to come out of the projects with your head on straight, but Kirby did. He played baseball almost every day through the summers, went to school and stayed out of trouble.

When asked what it was like growing up in Chicago, Kirby replied, "It was hard but I had to be very strong."

He attended Triton Junior College in River Grove, Illinois. Puckett didn't have the chiseled body of a classic athlete. When a pro scout came to watch his team play, the scout was looking at someone else. But it was the hard-working hustle of Kirby Puckett that won the Twins representative's attention.

In the first round of the January 1982 Free Agent Draft, the Minnesota Twins took the outfielder from Chicago. Kirby would spend his entire career in a Twins uniform. His play would directly correspond to the glory days of Minnesota baseball as Puckett helped deliver two world championships.

His stay in the minor leagues was a short one. On May 8, 1984, Kirby made his major-league debut against the California Angels. His first game was just a hint of what was to come. The rookie rapped out four hits in that game.

Many memorable games would follow in his twelve years in major-league baseball, and the only game that made him nervous was Game One of the 1987 World Series. On August 30, 1987, Kirby lashed out six hits for fourteen total bases in a game at Milwaukee. The next day he was four-for-five, an amazing ten-for-eleven streak.

Game Six of the 1987 World Series saw Puckett go four-for-four. Even so, it was four years later in Game Six of the 1991 World Series that stamped greatness and Kirby Puckett firmly into the minds of millions of baseball fans.

The Twins jumped ahead of the Braves two games to none playing at the Metrodome. Big trouble struck the Twins in Atlanta. They dropped three in a row.

The Twins returned home on the brink of disaster. One loss and the series would be over. Puckett told his teammates, "Jump on my back, and I'll carry you." He wasn't kidding.

The Twins took an early 2-0 lead in the first inning. In the second inning, with a runner on base, the Braves' Ron Gant lofted a drive deep to left center field. Kirby raced back to the Plexiglas fence and timed his leap perfectly. Gant's drive slapped into Kirby's glove, robbing him of an extra-base hit and the Braves of at least one run.

Finally, in the bottom of the eleventh, Puckett's third hit of the game—the homer off Leibrandt—sent Twins' fans home deliriously happy.

The next night Minnesota won their second baseball world championship with a thrilling 1-0 extra inning victory. When asked what he remembers best, Kirby replied, "We won!"

Kirby Puckett continued to make baseball history for the Twins for the next four years as he excited crowds at bat and in the field. Then, baseball fans got a big scare at the end of the 1995 season when Kirby was hit near his left eye by a pitched ball in the last series of the season.

Relief that the injury wouldn't end Kirby's playing days was short-lived. On March 28, 1996, during spring training season in Fort Myers, Florida, Kirby awoke with blurred vision in his right eye. It was diagnosed as glaucoma, unrelated to his injury. Later that summer, Puckett was forced to announce his retirement from active play because of irreversible damage to his right retina, but he feels now that it was time to move on with his life.

Puckett was active in the Twins' front office as an executive vice-president, with responsibilities including team strategy, player evaluation and recruiting, and individual player instruction, along with working as an instructor in the minor-league system.

Kirby still is very involved in community affairs. He was awarded the 1996 Roberto Clemente Man of the Year Award by Major League Baseball for his outstanding community service and the Branch Rickey Community Service Award.

Kirby's greatest personal honor came on January 16, 2001, when he was elected on the first ballot to the Baseball Hall of Fame in Cooperstown, New York.

Wherever he goes, Kirby is still the subject of adoration from fans who remember the smiling, determined ball player who made watching baseball fun and exciting in Minnesota.

He was dedicated to winning but never forgot the people for whom he was playing: the fans.

The *Minneapolis Star-Tribune* named Puckett "Minnesota's Most Important Sports Figure of the Twentieth Century."

Together with his wife, Tonya, and their children, Catherine and Kirby, Jr., Kirby lives in Edina, Minnesota.

Kirby's advice for school children is "always follow your dreams and live for today." He also believes that pro-ball players owe it to the community to help make things better. He believes that for baseball to improve, the teams must all play at the same level.

Source: Minnesota-Twins-provided biographical material. *2000 Twins Media Guide.*

Harold Stassen
Governor and Statesman

Governor Harold E. Stassen's legacy to Minnesotans is peace and foresight. A truly visionary leader, this Minnesotan looked beyond state and national boundaries to recognize our world as a global community back in the 1930s.

Stassen worked with powerful world figures such as President Franklin D. Roosevelt, British Prime Minister Winston Churchill, French President Charles DeGaulle, and Soviet Premier Josef Stalin, as he accepted challenges, including helping to draft the United Nations Charter.

Stassen was born on April 13, 1907, on a farm in Dakota County, Minnesota. As a child, his father, William, instilled in him a sense of community pride and commitment. Harold traveled with his father to civic meetings and Republican political gatherings. The young man took dedication to the people to heart.

Harold applied that sense of dedication towards his own education. He was eleven years old when he entered St. Paul Humboldt High School; four years later, he graduated sixth in his class. Just fifteen, Stassen advanced to college and law school at the University of Minnesota, finishing in six years. He was admitted to the Minnesota Bar at age twenty-one.

Soon afterward, he married childhood friend Esther Glewwe. Then public service called. He was elected Dakota County Attorney at age twenty-three.

For the next eight years, Stassen established his reputation for being tough on crime—a reputation that was to lead him to the governorship.

The 1930s saw hard times in Minnesota as well as the nation; poverty and despair gripped everyone. This led to labor strikes and violent demonstrations. Gangsters like John Dillinger called St. Paul home, with little resistance from the police force. Prohibition of alcohol led to bootlegging. With few options, many people turned to crime. County Attorney Stassen rose to the forefront in prosecuting the lawless.

When he ran for governor of Minnesota, Stassen's campaign offered a new, progressive Republicanism. He claimed that his administration would be free of corruption and Communism.

In 1938, Stassen became the youngest governor ever elected in America. The thirty-one-year old gained sixty-five percent of the vote with his promise to reform government.

His accomplishments were impressive; among them were Minnesota's first civil service law, development of an industry mining low-grade iron ore, equalization of tax assessments, improvement of Social Security benefits, and a labor conciliation law.

As a Progressive Republican, Stassen didn't try to dismantle Roosevelt's New Deal. Rather, he attempted to manage the programs with greater efficiency. One of his greatest contributions was the modernization of state government. Stassen's civil service reform destroyed patronage and political machines.

In 1940, he gave the keynote address at the Republican National Convention, speaking of "Enlightened Capitalism." Stassen was overwhelmingly re-elected governor in 1940 and again in 1942. He had promised when he ran for re-election that he would leave office after the legislative session was completed and the legislation had been disposed. He then entered the navy for service in World War II.

That decision landed Stassen aboard the *U.S.S. Missouri*, where he served as aide to famed naval hero Admiral William Halsey, the Commander of the Third Fleet in the Pacific during World War II. Stassen was at Halsey's side when the admiral issued momentous orders that brought victory at the Battle of Leyte Gulf, the largest naval battle in history in terms of tonnage.

Stassen and Halsey were standing on the *Missouri's* bridge when an officer rushed forward with a special alert: the Japanese forces were at the north edge of the Philippines.

"Run at top speed," Halsey ordered, "and sink those carriers at dawn!"

The mission was successful. Halsey's Third Fleet scored a decisive victory at Leyte Gulf. Joined by Admiral Thomas Kincaid's Seventh Fleet, Halsey's fleet smashed the Japanese navy, virtually eliminating it from World War II.

One of Stassen's finest moments came at the end of the war when Halsey assigned him to help supervise "Operation Benevolence," the rescue of 14,000 American prisoners of war from the Japanese home islands.

Knowing his stand opposed to isolationism, President Franklin Roosevelt appointed Naval Commander Stassen to be one of eight delegates to the founding conference of the United Nations in San Francisco. Then in his late thirties,

Stassen worked tirelessly to make the United Nations a reality. He was highly impressed with the world leaders with whom he worked.

His work with the United Nations included arranging a compromise with Josef Stalin of the Soviet Union. Reporters from around the globe who covered the Charter proceedings named Stassen and an Australian diplomat as the two most effective contributors to the signing of the United Nations Charter.

In 1948, after returning to Minnesota, Stassen ran for the Republican nomination for president of the United States. He lost a hard-fought battle to New York Governor Thomas Dewey, who eventually was upset by President Harry Truman.

The words of this popular former governor continued to carry great weight. In various speeches, Stassen spoke of the need to end isolationism and of the necessity for America to involve itself in future world peace.

Harold and Esther Stassen and their two children, Glen and Kathleen, moved to Pennsylvania so he could serve as p resident of the University of Pennsylvania. There he worked in academic areas while encouraging General Dwight Eisenhower, at that time NATO's Supreme Commander in Europe, to seek the Republican nomination for the 1952 presidential election.

As Eisenhower hesitated, Stassen offered himself as a candidate once again to stave off isolationist candidates and keep the field open for the general. The strategy worked. Eisenhower entered the race and defeated Senator Taft on the first convention ballot, with Minnesota's ballots clinching the nomination.

Stassen served Eisenhower in cabinet-level positions for the next five years. He became the director of foreign operations and used his assignments to promote his visions for world peace. His admiration of Eisenhower was prevalent as he continued to work toward his ideals. He outlined basics to break the stalemate of the Cold War. In 1951, he correctly predicted the "coming collapse of Communism."

Stassen also served Eisenhower on the National Security Council and as a special assistant to the president for disarmament policy.

He left the cabinet in 1958 and established a private law office in Philadelphia. There he lost races for governor of Pennsylvania and mayor of Philadelphia.

Stassen continued to speak out for world peace and on the issues that concerned his country. When President Johnson said the war could be won in one hundred days, Stassen warned he wouldn't win in "one hundred times one hundred days." Governor Stassen urged that Johnson not escalate the war.

At the Republican Convention in 1968, Stassen, again a presidential candidate, warned that if the United States simply pulled out, the Communists would slaughter the loyal Vietnamese. He added that, if the war continued, many more lives would be lost, and that the war could not be won. Stassen encouraged the United States to take a strong defensive posture, making occasional offensive strikes to maintain their position, and to train Vietnamese troops to fight their own war.

His name was placed in nomination for the presidency at that convention by his nephew, J. Robert Stassen of Minnesota, who also helped to place a plank in the Republican Platform, which contained many of his uncle's positions on the war.

In his many subsequent campaigns for president, Stassen used the electioneering platform to keep his ideas before the public.

Harold and Esther Stassen moved back to Minnesota in 1978. Harold returned to the practice of law and maintained an interest in Minnesota politics.

Esther passed away on October 7, 2000, at age ninety-four. The Stassens had been married seventy years. Their daughter, Kathleen Stassen Berger, commented, "She gave us an example of how to build and sustain a marriage over a long, long time despite all the things that happened. Their love for each other was and is incredible."

Still a visionary in his later years, the former governor recently wondered why some of his suggestions hadn't taken hold. "Don't you think that a canal connecting Lake Superior to the Mississippi River would be a good idea?" he asked.

Harold Stassen continued to look to the possibilities in our future. His advice to today's school children is to "study carefully and aim high."

Note: As this book went to press, Harold Stassen passed away on March 4, 2001, at the age of ninety-three.

Sources: Author's personal interview; biographical material provided by subject; *Minnesota, A History of the State*, Theodore Blegen, University of Minnesota Press, Minneapolis, 1963.

Will Steger
Explorer and Educator

Growing up in Minnesota, it's natural for a child to be fond of snow and ice. Minnesota kids thrive in the cold. They sled, skate, ski, snowmobile, and otherwise frolic in the fluffy white stuff.

Will Steger carried this play to a very serious extreme. He became an explorer of the Earth's North and South Poles.

Born August 27, 1944, in St. Paul, Steger spent his growing-up years in Richfield. From a young age, Will was fascinated by the polar regions. He also had an intense desire to explore and to see things that few before him had seen. This fascination led Will to become America's foremost explorer, educator, photographer, writer, and lecturer on the poles.

Steger's first exploration occurred when he was only fifteen and one-half years old. He and his brother Tom traveled the Mississippi River by motorboat from Minneapolis to New Orleans.

For the next decade, Steger combined his education with travels. He remained in his home state to attend the College of St. Thomas (now a university), earning a bachelor's degree in geology in 1966 and a master's in education in 1969. However, he capitalized on summer breaks to satisfy his desire to learn from personal exploration. From 1963 to 1970, he traveled 10,000 miles by kayak in northern rivers including the MacKenzie, Peace, and Yukon rivers in Canada.

Will combined some mountain climbing with his other adventures, too. In 1962, he climbed Mt. Rainier in Washington, and in 1965, he went 20,585 up Peru's Pelcaraju.

When he was nineteen, one of Will's explorations took him to Minnesota's Boundary Waters Canoe Area. He fell in love with a patch of wilderness and made a fifty-dollar down payment on it. Steger dubbed the site "The Homestead." It would become his future home and base of operations.

For three years he taught science at St. Richard's School in Minneapolis. But the call to explore and live in the wilds remained strong. In 1970 Steger left Minneapolis and moved to the wilderness north of Ely, Minnesota, back to "The Homestead."

In northern Minnesota, he established a winter school and, for ten years, pioneered outdoor programs using dog teams and skis as a means of travel.

In 1982, Will Steger began seriously to put into practice what he had been teaching and training. He began an eighteen-month, 6,000-mile dog sled expedition that took him throughout Canada's Northwest Territories and Alaska.

This was followed in 1985 by a 5,000-mile dog sled journey from Ely to Barrow, Alaska.

The harshness and frigid cold of the poles required the explorers to modify their eating and sleeping habits. Will said, "We usually cooked breakfast and supper. We only had like ten- to twenty-minute breaks for lunch, since stopping for too long meant getting cold. We ate pasta, rice, butter, pemmican, nuts, and oatmeal. Not bulky stuff since weight is a major consideration. We slept very well. We'd do ten-hour, sometimes twelve-hour days of skiing and running. Our bodies were exhausted, and sleep is a very good way of rejuvenating."

Sponsors like GoreTex, Shaklee, and NorthFace gave money to help the explorers meet their goals without worrying about supplies.

The lure of lands farther north kept calling Will. He launched upon his history-making polar expedition in 1986. He led a team of six to the North Pole by dog sled. It was the first recorded unsupported expedition to the pole. For fifty-five arduous days they zigzagged a thousand miles, crossed the Arctic Ocean, braved pack ice as it threatened to break apart under them, and endured frigid temperatures approaching seventy degrees below zero.

But they made it!

Just two years later he outdid himself. Steger led the longest unsupported dog sled journey in history. He and his team traveled 1,600 miles, doing a south-north traverse of Greenland.

The trips were just the beginning for the explorer. Will put together an international team of six and led them on another history-making expedition. This time they would brave deep crevasses, the most dangerous part of all of Will's journeys, and forty-degree-below-zero temperatures as they made the first dog sled traverse of Antarctica, the South Pole.

The International Trans-Antarctica Expedition traveled 3,741 miles across the frozen continent from 1989 to 1990. Following the journey, Steger met with

President George Bush, Sr., and leaders from France, the Soviet Union, Japan, and China to discuss the preservation of Antarctica.

Ever concerned with education, the environment, and exploration, Steger combined the three to reach beyond just going where few had gone before. His goal was to draw attention to the polar regions and the need to preserve them. He wanted to draw particular attention to the South Pole, where the possibility of mining oil and minerals deep below the ice could threaten the continent's ecosystem.

Steger had one more major expedition in mind, the International Ice Project. This would entail a 1,200-mile crossing of the Arctic Ocean from Russia to Ellesmere Island, Canada. From 1992 to 1994, Will led three training expeditions in northern Canada to prepare for the crossing.

The International Ice Project was successfully completed in 1995. As with the Trans-Antarctic expedition of 1990, the crossing of the Arctic Ocean set milestones in telecommunications. Both expeditions shared their experiences with the world through computer hookups and the Internet.

Even though he officially left the teaching profession in 1970, Will Steger remained very much an educator, strongly believing that a better understanding is essential regarding humanity's role and impact on the environment.

To that end, Steger founded the Global Center of Environmental Education at Minnesota's Hamline University in 1991, and the World School for Adventure Learning at his alma mater, the University of St. Thomas, in 1993.

To further knowledge of the environment and the poles, Steger has testified twice before Congress, written four books and frequently lectured.

Will's articles and photographs have appeared in *National Geographic Magazine* and numerous other publications.

The polar explorer's courage and dedication to the cause of furthering environmental understanding have received numerous honors. He is one of only nineteen people to receive the prestigious National Geographic Society's John Oliver La Gorce Medal since the society was founded in 1888. Amelia Earhart, Robert Peary, and Jacques Cousteau were among those honored. In 1995, Will Steger was added to this distinguished list of great explorers.

In 1997, he planned a solo expedition of the North Pole. Six days into the mission, he called it off. While camped on an ice flow in sub-zero temperatures, Will realized that he could get into a situation where the lives of others could be in peril while attempting to rescue him. He was prepared to risk his own life but not others'.

Throughout his career, Steger has been aware that in order for Antarctica and the environment to be saved, people must be informed. His expeditions educate, as do his lectures and writings.

Even in his earliest explorations, Will sensed the need to record and communicate. Going online with school children and others interested in his exploits has been an important part of his mission.

For a year and one-half in the late 1990s, Will explored northern Minnesota and southern Ontario. His observations were recorded in a "Wilderness Journal" that was available to students and others over the Internet.

Elmer L. Andersen, former Minnesota governor and a newspaper editor, interviewed Steger. In his column, he described his meeting with Will. "His demeanor was serious, but occasionally a warm open smile brightened his countenance. One could not help but be drawn to him and his cause in complete confidence; he has that mystical magnetism of the true leader."

Will and his wife, Elsa, continued to live north of Ely in the Minnesota forests. At that time he had no plans for more big expeditions, but he did expect to revisit the North Pole from time to time with friends. Maybe Minnesota winters are just too warm.

Will's advice to school children is, "Education is very important. Study hard and follow your dreams."

Sources: Biographical information provided by subject; *North to the Pole* by Will Steger, Times Books, New York, 1987.

Bobby Vee
Singer

Sometimes even tragedy has a silver lining. For many people, February 3, 1959, is "the day the music died." A light plane named "American Pie" went down near Clear Lake, Iowa, ending the lives of three of rock music's greatest young superstars, Buddy Holly, Richie Valens, and the Big Bopper (J. P. Richardson).

Hundreds of miles north, in the Fargo-Moorhead region, another young life would be impacted greatly by the crash. In another way, music would be born.

Robert Velline (Bobby Vee) was born in Fargo, North Dakota, on April 30, 1943. His family was very musical. His father, Sidney, played the violin and piano; Siama, his mother, had a beautiful singing voice; and Bobby's two older brothers, Bill and Sidney, Jr., both played guitar.

Bobby played saxophone in his high-school band, but it was rock 'n' roll music that captured his imagination. Brother Bill and his friends, Jim Stillman and Bob Korum, formed a "garage band," and Bobby kind of weaseled his way into their sessions. It helped that he had saved thirty dollars from his paper route to buy a guitar and that he knew the words to the songs they were playing.

Bobby was a sophomore in Fargo High School on February 3, 1959. He was home from school on a lunch break when his brother Sid told him about the news flash that Buddy and the others had died.

Holly was Bobby's idol. The sophomore had all of Buddy's records and knew most of his songs. In fact, he had a ticket for a show that was to be given by Buddy in neighboring Moorhead, Minnesota, that very night.

Moorhead had been the ill-fated plane's destination. Interspersed with the news accounts of the stars' deaths was a call for local acts to perform in the Moorhead Armory that night.

The promoters were determined to have a show and needed fill-ins to supplement the remaining acts. Jim Stillman called radio station KFGO, and at 7:00 p.m. fifteen-year-old Bobby and his friends were backstage. Their band didn't even have a name.

The master of ceremonies of the event was a local radio star, Charlie Boone. Bobby later recalled, "Charlie did a masterful job of presenting what would seem like an impossible evening. No one else seemed to know what to say or how to say it."

A couple of acts performed. Bill Velline realized that he didn't have a guitar strap, so he borrowed one from Dion of Dion and The Belmonts. When Boone called for them, they scrambled onstage, "knees knocking."

Charlie asked, "What's the name of the band?"

Bobby thought a moment and improvised, "the Shadows." Then they begin to sing. While Bobby knew all of Holly's songs, they sang none of them that night.

The Shadows were well received. Charlie introduced them to his agent, Bing Bengtssen, who offered to represent them. They talked with Boone and Bengtssen about how to make a record and get started in the business.

Boone recalled, "We didn't know he would be a star that night, but it was obvious that he had talent. Bobby was a terrific kid, a real gentleman from the start. He was unlike many of the rock singers that came through at that time."

The Shadows made sixty dollars in their first paying performance on Valentine's Day of 1959. They were on their way. On June 1, the group went to Minneapolis, Minnesota, where they recorded a song written by Bobby for Soma Records. "Susie Baby" became a big regional hit and attracted the attention of national record companies. That fall, the Shadows signed with Liberty Records.

But the music business was tough and national hit records hard to come by. By late 1960, only a couple of Bobby's records had inched their way onto the charts.

Liberty appeared to be preparing to drop the Shadows when a radio station in Pittsburgh began to play the flip side of Bobby's last release.

"Devil or Angel" was to peak at number six in the Billboard charts and re-establish Bobby Vee as an emerging star. Liberty re-signed Bobby to a five-year contract.

Soon the young singer would be performing before 110,000 people at Lake Pontchartrain, Louisiana, alongside the likes of Roy Orbison and the Everly Brothers.

Over the next thirty-plus years of performing, Bobby would have thirty-eight songs in Billboard's Top 100 charts, six gold singles, fourteen Top 40 hits, and two gold albums.

The Shadows continued as a band until 1963, when Bill, tiring of a life of travel, left to work closer to home. But Bobby was just beginning.

People the world over were rocking to the sounds of "Rubber Ball" and "The Night Has a Thousand Eyes." Bobby had seven Top 10 hits in England as well as a number-two album entitled "Bobby Vee Meets the Crickets."

For forty weeks in 1963, he shared space on the charts with the Beatles. Bobby toured Japan, Australia, and much of Europe. He still tours the United Kingdom each year.

His twenty-five-plus albums include a Gold Album from England for his 1981 "Singles Album." *Billboard* magazine has called Bobby, "One of the top ten most consistent chart makers ever."

Vee continues to brighten lives with his music. He continued to base his operation near St. Cloud, Minnesota, where he has his own studio, Rockhouse Productions. He and his wife, Karen, live at nearby St. Joseph.

A native of North Dakota, Bobby always considered Minnesota his second home. His family vacationed at the lakes of the North Star State when he was a youth.

Bobby still performs over one hundred engagements a year. He takes added pride in that his three sons, Jeff, Tom, and Robb, have started working with him in the band. Daughter Jennifer, a graphic designer with Sassafrass Designs in Minneapolis, adds her creative touch when studio artwork is needed.

Bobby's high-energy performances have kept him in the public eye. *The Beat Goes On*, a '60s music magazine, voted him multiple honors: 1991 Best American Act; 1992 Best Live Performer; 1993 Favorite Male Singer; and, in 1994, Runner-Up to Paul McCartney as Most Accomplished Performer. *The Beat Goes On* also voted him as Number One International Act.

In September of 1995, and again in 1997, Bobby was honored to appear in London to celebrate McCartney's "Buddy Holly Week." Carl Perkins and the Crickets and former Beatles member Paul McCartney performed along with Bobby. In June of 1996, Vee performed at Andrew Lloyd Webber's Sydmonton Festival. The English connections have been kind to Bobby.

It has been a rich career for the boy from Fargo. Bobby's fifteenth birthday found him struggling to get his brothers to let him play in their band. By his sixteenth birthday, he had recorded a hit record and was celebrating his party live on the radio from the Moonlight Drive-In in Fargo, courtesy of Charlie Boone.

Who knows, if his hero's "American Pie" hadn't crashed on that frigid February night in Iowa, Bobby's life might have taken another turn; he might, in his words, "Be in Cornwall painting pictures of old England. Or possibly I'd still be standing on the corner selling the *Fargo Forum*."

Bobby's advice for school children is, "Follow the Golden Rule and listen to your heart. Maybe the greatest gift of all is to know and trust in your heart, know what works for you. Honesty starts with ourselves. Paint your picture to your liking. Sing your song, to your liking. Always strive to be as good as you can be and learn from your mistakes."

"One of the songs that I have continually enjoyed singing is 'More Than I Can Say' written by Jerry Allison and Sonny Curtis of Buddy Holly's Crickets. It was a minor hit for me in America but a top ten international hit in Australia, England, and China. Traveling around the world, as I do, I've had the opportunity to experience the impact that American music has had on the rest of the world. I am continually reminded that, in spite of the many different languages or the colors of our skin, when it comes to matters of the heart we are all very much the same. Music brings people together."

Bobby has written about one hundred songs and recorded maybe half of those. His music writes itself, however. He sits with a guitar and lets the music and words unfold. "I've learned over the years not to judge it but rather work with whatever comes." Some of his songs come from his life, especially those about relationships.

Sources: Personal phone interview by author; Bobby Vee's website.

Jesse Ventura
Entertainer and Governor

On November 3, 1998, Jesse Ventura—former professional wrestler, actor, and talk-show host—in his own words, "Shocked the world!" He was elected governor of Minnesota, the only Reform Party candidate in America to ever win statewide office.

The road to the governor's mansion on Summit Avenue in St. Paul took many twists and turns before anyone stamped the name "Jesse Ventura" on the mailbox.

Governor Ventura was born James Janos on July 15, 1951, to George Janos, an army veteran and steam fitter for the city of Minneapolis, and First Lieutenant Bernice Janos, a nurse-anesthetist.

As a child, Jesse admired Mohammad Ali.

Jesse grew up in the south Minneapolis Longfellow neighborhood, attended Cooper Elementary School, and graduated from Roosevelt Senior High School in 1969.

After high school, he followed his brother into the navy and was trained as a S.E.A.L. Jesse served his country in the navy for six years, with four on active duty, including a tour in Vietnam, and two years of reserves.

He attended North Hennepin Community College on the GI Bill in 1973 but left after only one year. The young Navy S.E.A.L. from south Minneapolis had decided to become a professional wrestler in the style of a man he had always admired, superstar Billy Graham.

Janos built up his already strong physique, changed his name to "Jesse" because he liked it, and added the glamorous surname "Ventura" from surf-side California. He had to reinvent himself for the ring, for pro wrestlers all had a "gimmick" of some sort. Thus, James Janos became "Surfer Jesse Ventura," the golden boy from California. But, in the eyes of wrestling fans, "Surfer" didn't fit the man. He soon became known as Jesse "The Body" Ventura.

He broke in under Vern Gagne in the American Wrestling Association (AWA). Ventura won a tag-team title with Adrian Adonis as part of the East-West connection.

After leaving the AWA for the World Wrestling Federation (WWF), Ventura had epic struggles with Hulk Hogan. Using the "bad" guy image, complete with feather boas, he was often matched against the popular Hogan. Jesse's flamboyant style and clothing, reminiscent of the legendary Gorgeous George, in addition to his raucous taunting of audiences and opponents, made him one of the most loved "bad guys" in wrestling.

Ventura's ring career came to an abrupt halt in 1987 when he developed blood clots in his lungs. He was advised that continued pounding in the "squared circle" could lead to a collapsed lung or other injuries. Jesse retired as an active athlete.

But he stayed in wrestling as a television color commentator with the WWF. Paired with Gorilla Monson as a co-host of *Prime Time Wrestling*, his popularity continued to grow.

The image Ventura had projected in the ring and on TV led to an acting career. He appeared in the movies *Predator*, his personal favorite, and *Batman and Robin* with Arnold Schwarzenegger, and made television appearances such as a guest spot on *The X Files*.

Ventura returned to wrestling as a commentator for World Championship Wrestling and did some color announcing for pro-football. But Jesse Ventura had his sights set on other goals.

In 1990, Jesse became embroiled in a fight to save a wetland in his town of Brooklyn Park, Minnesota. He felt that city government was indifferent to his concerns and literally took on City Hall. He was elected mayor that year in one of the biggest election turnouts in recent Brooklyn Park history. He governed the city until 1995, championing crime reduction. Then he left office and moved outside the city limits, near Maple Grove, to live on a horse farm with his wife, Terry, and children, Tyrel and Jade. The former wrestler also served as volunteer assistant football coach at Champlin Park High School, specializing in strength training.

Jesse kept his voice and opinions before the public as a talk show host. First, he worked at KSTP-AM and then KFAN-AM Radio. He used these shows to expound on his general beliefs that too much government is bad and to focus on his personal interests.

Jesse wanted lower license fees and no tampering with his personal water-craft rights. From these public forums, people became more acquainted with his no-nonsense, fiscally conservative, socially moderate views.

In 1998 he became the Reform Party's candidate for governor of Minnesota. Initially it appeared to be a joke—a former pro-wrestler running for the highest office in the state. But his time as mayor of Brooklyn Park made him credible to many, and his ideas and blunt talk carried wide appeal, especially for young males.

Political organizers, whose task it is to drum up crowds for candidate appearances, know that's a tough job. Newspaper ads, phone calls, and personal contacts might get a couple dozen people to attend an event early in a campaign.

That made a summer appearance in Litchfield all the more impressive. Jesse Ventura strode into the local VFW Hall to find it crowded with a couple hundred people. Little, if any, phoning had been done. One very small notice had appeared in the town paper.

The candidate was wearing a baseball cap, blue jeans, and t-shirt, not the customary suit of a politician. He spoke directly and forthrightly, answered questions and joked for over two hours. Ventura captivated his audience. No one left the hall. This was different. So different that Jesse Ventura surprised everyone, except maybe himself, on November 3, 1998, by beating the Republican mayor of St. Paul, Norm Coleman and the DFL Attorney General Hubert Humphrey III. He "shocked the world." Jesse said that he had every intention of winning, otherwise he would not have run for governor.

Jesse says that although both wrestling and politics require both strategy and thought, they are not the same at all.

As governor, Jesse is credited with surrounding himself with good people and making excellent appointments to his staff. He presided over the single greatest tax rebate in Minnesota history.

Governor Ventura has pushed for a unicameral legislature and a light-rail transit system. He has traveled to Japan on a trade mission and has made numerous national public appearances.

Ventura wrote a book about his life story, *I Ain't Got Time to Bleed*, taking the title from his famous line in the movie, *Predator*.

His interviews and appearances have often led to colorful and provocative remarks. In spite of what some believed were controversial comments by Ventura, at mid-term his popularity level was the highest measured in state history.

In February of 2000, Governor Ventura left the Reform Party. Concerned with the direction in which presidential candidate Patrick Buchanen and party founder Ross Perot were taking the party, he became an Independent.

In February 2001, Jesse made his debut as a television analyst for the XFL Football League. The XFL is a professional football league owned by NBC Television and the World Wrestling Federation.

Ventura's participation in the league led to controversy and charges of trading upon his position as governor. But Jesse maintained his right to do what he wants with his spare time.

In many ways, Jesse's fight to maintain his rights and the rights of his family have been under fire throughout his term in office. He says that the worst thing about being governor is giving up his personal freedom, not being able to run out to the store without a full security detail. However, for Jesse, the best thing is to be the boss and not have anyone able to tell him what to do. Jesse has upheld his notion that his family need not be involved in his political career, something he believes is paramount.

Jesse says he has no plans to run for president of the United States. He says he would never put his family through such an ordeal.

In almost every sense, Jesse Ventura has lived his life to the fullest, a life truly larger than most in many respects. His advice for school children is to get involved and make a difference.

In response to school children's questions regarding his appearance, he says that he started shaving his head several years ago and shaves it every morning.

Sources: Governor Jesse Ventura Website; author's insights and contacts.

About the Author

Dean Urdahl is a native of Litchfield, Minnesota. He graduated from St. CLoud State University in 1971, and has taught American History in New London-Spicer (Minnesota) schools since that time.

Dean married Karen Frantti of St. Cloud, Minnesota, in 1971. They have three sons: Chad, sports editor of the *Owatonna People's Press*, and Brent and Troy, Spring 2001 graduates of Hamline University in St. Paul.

The Urdahls reside on a hobby farm in Meeker County. Dean's varied interests have led to involvement in many areas, including politics, education, government, sports, and writing. He has been a devoted fan of the Minnesota Twins since childhood.

Dean and Karen have derived much enjoyment watching their athletic sons compete in sports at the high-school and college levels over the years. Dean is still an avid softball and basketball player, while Karen enjoys walking.

All members of the family have worked with Urdahl Paint Company, a business started by Dean's father, Clarence, fifty years ago. Dean has another book, *Touching Bases with Our Memories*, which features famous living former Minnesota Twins players, forthcoming from North Star Press. He is currently editing his novel on the Dakota Conflict.

New London-Spicer Class of 2005

Derek Amundson	Nick Dahlen	Benjamin Bonnema	Alyscia Binnebose	Daniel Bengtson	Michael Dahl
Christopher Baxter	Ben Dahmes	Joshua Chapin	Maggie Campe	Desarae Clark	Christopher
Christopher Beckrich	Darren Gau	Lori Chastek	Allison Deadrick	Ashley Eliason	Goeddertz
Heather Christensen	Paul Giroux	Laura Christensen	Calli Decathelineau	Kristin Erickson	Tara Hagen
Ashley Christianson	Kari Haug	Brittany Connor	Jennifer Ditmarson	Heather Fredeen	Benjamin Hanson
Jessie Ekstrom	Sarah Hengel	Jade Cooley	Michael Field	Adam Gorecki	Jeremy Harder
Ashley Evans	Jennifer	Hailey Edwards	Jordan Geister	Jessica Heinen	Mitchell Keenan
Amanda Fauchald	Hoffenkamp	Cody Johanson	Deserae	Logan Kalkbrenner	Robert Keller
Daniel Fultz	Amanda Johnson	Benjamin Johnson	Grafenstein	Kevin Krupke	Justin Kemppainen
Carrie Halliday	David Johnson	Janile Lewis	Janessa Gronli	Benjamin Kulset	John Kennedy
Levi Hood	Kayla Karnes	Sean Murphy	Anna Hoffman	Jessica Mueller	Ingrid Moulton
Beth Imdieke	Janell Kelley	Amber Nelson	Collin Kohls	Brent Nelson	Dennis Nazarenus
Ryan Jenniges	Alex Krick	Shane Nelson	Cody Leukam	Alex Neumann	Renee Noyes
Mark Juhl	Travis Lucas	Douglas Orlowski	Christopher	Erin Olson	Jenna Nygaard
Nathan Larsen	Daniel Millard	Zach Pederson	Lindquist	Adam Peterson	Eric Oss
Christopher Mehr	Lisa Mohrmann	Christopher Person	Tommy Moen	Mike Pickard	Eric Pederson
Jeremy Meis	Andrew Nelson	Kayla Powers	Emily Munyon	Kayla Richards	Ashley Raddatz
Sarah Nestande	Sarah Nordby	Matthew Robison	Wade Quisberg	Christopher Roelofs	Jessica Roth
Scott Rambow	Brady Pearson	Stephanie Sapp	Landis Reich	Jacob Sanderson	Amberly Samuelson
Nicholas Rogalski	Gary Peterson	Mark Skinelien	Casey Schmidt	David Sawatzky	Kari Stai
Bo Sjoberg	Marie Rindahl	Paul Skyora	Adam Schwalbe	Joshua Stulen	Charles Wallace
Dustin Torkelson	Ashley Schaeffer	Natasha Tabrizi	Rory Stierler	Mattea Thuney	Katie Wendlandt
Andrew Vogt	Jeron Smith	Megan Urban	Ryan Sundstrom	Josie Viessman	Justin Ziemer
Miranda Wig	Amber Strom	Jacob Wangen	Meghan Sykora	David Werner	
Amber Ziemer	Amanda Welker	Kimberly Arends	Danielle Thompson	Dustin Aalderks	
Alexander Brinton	Alexandra Bonham	Kari Barber	Kayla Timm	Logan Asche	